Trust in your innate goodness,
your heart, and every part of
your whole path.

Flourish

A 365-Day Guided Path Towards Love

HOW TO EXPERIENCE MORE JOY, LIVE WITH MORE
INTENTION, AND BE TRUE TO YOURSELF

ALLISON MCCABE BRUCE

Published by Flourish Integral Health

https://www.flourishintegralhealth.com

allison@flourishintegralhealth.com

Made in the USA

First Edition | Published 2022

Every reasonable attempt has been made to identify owners of copyright. Errors or omissions will be corrected in subsequent editions of the book.

The content of this book includes the beliefs of the author and is for informational purposes only. It is not intended to diagnose, treat, cure, or prevent any specific condition or disease and is not a substitute for consultation with a licensed professional. Please consult with your own physician or healthcare specialist regarding the suggestions and recommendations made in this book. If you are experiencing mental health challenges, seek quality care. The use of this book implies your acceptance of this disclaimer.

ISBN: 979-8-218-05395-6

Copy Editor: Rosie Accola

Graphic Artist: Jenn Kippert

Illustrator: Libby Ozog

Author Photos: Nicole Thomas Photography, Glenview, IL

Library of Congress Control Number: 2022918293

Name: Bruce, Allison McCabe, author

Name: Kippert, Jenn, illustrator

Name: Ozog, Libby, illustrator

Title: Flourish, a 365-day guided path towards love: how to experience more joy, live with more intention, and be true to yourself

Welcoming Gratitude

I am grateful to you, my reader. Amongst the hundreds of millions of published books, you have chosen to open your mind, body, and spirit to *Flourish*. I am honored to enter your life and share my truth. I hope the reflection guides you to realize your truth. The world becomes a much better place when we all are collectively living in our truth.

Every relationship that we have in our lives – our contact with each person, place, and event – serves a very special, if yet to be realized purpose: They are mirrors that can serve to show us things about ourselves that can be realized in no other way.

-GUY FINLEY

{ finds joy in personal growth }

Love

↑

Eternity

Water Rest Area

Picnic Rest Area

Vista Rest Area

CONTENTS

When you wish someone joy, you wish them peace, love, prosperity, happiness...all the good things.

- MAYA ANGELOU

{ found joy in advocating }

My Intentions

AN INTRODUCTION TO THE GUIDED PATH

Flourish, A 365-Day Guided Path Towards Love is a personal growth guidebook to help you get from where you are to where you want to be. The journey takes place in an enchanted forest imbued with the spirit of wisdom, decorated with navigational mile-marker lantern posts, and is intended to propel healing. Why design such a whimsical backdrop? The charming metaphorical setting represents our eternal magic, sparks our imagination, and expands our perspective. Offering a vibrant connection to your limitless creative superpower, this workbook serves as a bright resource to help you realize your true desires.

The guided path is my art of healing and living authentically after experiencing suffering and a spiritual awakening. A wide terrain of topics and strategies are covered over the course of the year we travel together. In both a pragmatic and artistic manner, I offer a life-changing formula of holistic health care perspectives, tools, and exercises you can easily implement in your daily life. The process can be applied to any physical, emotional, mental, or spiritual situation. I hope the concepts will help you better attune to your heart's innate wisdom, give yourself permission to change what you want to reframe, and consciously create the life you want to live.

Mostly prescriptive, part memoir, I begin with my story that led me to learn about the power of joy, and share about the magic following joy offers. Then we are onto the healing power of intention and the benefits intentional living can provide for your entire being. Holding the two essential keys of joy and intention, you set into motion a 365-day inner journey of self-realization. Each monthly chapter starts a brief meditation taking you further on your journey. The setting comes to life as you collect and employ each chapter's illuminated practices and walk the path towards your whole heart.

If you desire to live more genuinely, empowered, and trusting in the process of transformation towards your highest self; or, if you lack fulfillment, struggle with physical health, anxiety/depression, or trauma - this book is written for you. My intention is that *Flourish* truly improves your destiny. My hope is that as you explore, you awaken to the vast and powerful love inside yourself. And, at the end of this journey, you are healthier and embracing your whole, true self.

To the mountains of joy ahead!

What if navigating the entire journey
is as simple as listening to your heart,
following your joy, and with clear intentions
expressing your true self?

{ I find joy in self-realization }

The Why and How of

Flourish

F*lourish, A 365-Day Guided Path Towards Love* is written in support of growing and striving to live in an awakened state. I share my story, and how I have transformed through despair, to provide light. Your story may sound symbolically similar, or it may involve different challenges. On a higher consciousness level, our stories are unified. We are all on the same journey learning about love, and our divine true nature. The *Flourish* journey is authored as a resource to reflect your everlasting brilliance.

To those of you reading who specifically feel a lack of light, or little hope, know that you can overcome anything. *There is a luminous path ahead of you, a flourishing path is within you.*

Flourish:
1. (verb) grow or develop in a healthy or vigorous way, especially as the result of a particulary favorable environment.
2. (noun) an instance of suddenly performing or developing in an impressively successful way.

- OXFORD DICTIONARY

Have the courage to follow your heart and intuition. They somehow already know what you truly want to become happy. Everything else is secondary.

- STEVE JOBS

{ found joy in innovation }

My icebreaker is heavy, mud for the lotus! Six years ago, at the age of 43, my inner light was dim. It was a period of intense suffering. I was experiencing post-traumatic stress disorder from energetic abuse by two health care practitioners, coupled with confusion regarding a Kundalini awakening. I was in an unhealthy marriage. I felt highly stressed and depleted by my career, and I had financial worries. Physical health concerns at this time included a lumpectomy and IBS. I desired *to feel whole.* I did not, yet, see how to unravel a tightly wound life that, at the core, was clouded with overwhelming uncertainty, anxiety, and pain. In hindsight, low self-worth and depression lingered too. Shame kept me bound and suffering, for the most part, silently. My perception was that I could not communicate how terrible I felt inside, as that would reveal the depth of my brokenness.

I was attempting to be perfect; I struggled with perfectionism. If you had seen my life during this year, you might have said it looked beautiful. I had a wonderful family, and fulfilling friendships. I lived in a lovely home, and I was successful in my career. I felt gratitude for the blessings in my life, but overshadowing the goodness was a hot inferno of burning discomfort that generated a continuous desire to fade away. In *The Three Marriages*, David Whyte writes about the three marriages we have throughout our life: the marriage we have with our partner, the marriage we have with our work, and the marriage we have with ourselves. [1] My partnership union and my work pillar were failing. The abuse I experienced, and the subsequent post-traumatic stress, distorted my connection to myself. The three pillars of my life were simultaneously crumbling. I had become so misaligned with my true self that I found myself demoralized.

When we deny the story, it defines us. When we own the story, we can write a brave new ending.

- BRENÉ BROWN

{ finds joy in researching wholeheartedness }

In a moment of desperation and suicidal ideation, I prayed to understand that life had purpose. I passionately called on God/Universe/Source/Higher Self and asked for a sign that would indicate we are spiritual beings having a human experience, and not the other way around. At that time, validating our spiritual existence was a means to comprehend how I was energetically abused, which had me questioning the nature of reality as I undersood it. Further, I wanted to make sense of life's pain, and trust that we are connected to something more powerful than our human selves.

My prayer was specific. I asked that either one of the two people who abused me would contact me within 10 minutes. I realize the thought of ending my life and my ask both read illogical. My mindset at the moment points to the degree of my post-traumatic stress, its toll on my mental health, and the dysfunction that results from exploitation. In hindsight, I now understand from a spiritual awakening perspective my ego identity was transforming. "A suicidal intention signals a point of surrender. It's the point at which the ego gives up and stops trying. It therefore represents a point of acceptance." [2] I share all this to add, quite remarkably, that within a few minutes I was given an equally specific answer to my prayer. A picture of a passage titled "Navigation" arrived in a text message from one of the two abusers. The passage read:

"When everything collapses around you and the footing beneath you crumbles, the heart panics. It is in those moments of confusion, loss and despair, that we feel the Illusion of Separation the most, plunged into the dark of our own deepest fears. The challenge in these moments is not to attempt to "overcome" the feeling consuming us, as the struggle against the churning and painful current will deplete what small emotional resources we do have left. The challenge is to relax into the current, floating atop the river outstretched in the sun, calmed by the faith that wherever the river is headed, it's had one million years to carve its journey along the way ---- and perhaps it knows where it's going." [3]

I received the sign that I asked for to confirm my existence, help make sense of my experiences, endure my pain, and know how powerful we all are. From here, overwhelmed with emotion, I vowed to reconstruct my life from the inside to feel whole. I view this as a moment of impact, *the point at which the light began to fill in the cracks.* As described in the movie *The Vow*, "The moment of impact provides potential for change. It has ripple effects far beyond what we can predict."

*Believe what your heart tells you when you ask, "Does this spark joy?"
If you act on that intuition, you will be amazed at how
things will begin to connect in your life and at the dramatic
changes that follow.*

- MARIE KONDO

{ finds joy in organizing }

Many miracles transpired shortly after my declaration. One was the arrival of a career coach and her suggestion to read *The Life-Changing Magic of Tidying Up* by Marie Kondo. This book did truly change my life. The premise of the book is to reset your life by decluttering. The key to the method is to only keep what "sparks joy" in you. As I decluttered my home, I began paying real attention to joy for the first time. Listening to my heart when I queried if something "sparked joy" helped me identify and sort, not just my physical possessions, but also my feelings and my life. I began to pause, honor the emotion in my heart, and follow its direction. I made more choices based on feeling versus thought. Decisions from my heart center felt noticeability lighter, and I perceived a newfound sense of ease in my life. I endearingly labeled these heartfelt moments *Project Joy*.

To carry *Project Joy* forward, and make the act of honoring joy more of an official adventure, I challenged myself to photograph and blog about the most joyful moment of each day for an entire year. (Yes, a tall New Year's intention!) Through this inspirational challenge, I hoped to find more love inside myself, in addition to inspiring others to look at their joy. Honoring the uneasiness that writing openingly was producing and knowing my intended writing practice was established, I stopped posting on day 43. (Frankly, the commitment to writing an open journal daily was causing night sweats!) However, I continued to write privately, and still do to this day. What began as a year-long project has become a lifetime dedication due to the strength that I continue to gain from invaluable insights. What I have learned, now in my sixth year, is that following joy provides a stream of courage to find your truth. It is a path to becoming your true self.

The second influential book recommended by my career coach was *The Artist's Way* by Julia Cameron. The book is a 12-week program of self-discovery dedicated to cultivating your creativity compassionately, and honoring your work as an expression of God/Universe/Source/Higher Self working through you. It was the foundational elements of *The Artist's Way*, the morning journaling pages and weekly artist dates, that had the most influence. I found journaling about my fears and dreams daily to be a healing process. With a newfound sense of self-reflection, I more confidently pursued going on weekly artist dates to explore my interests. Some interests were packed away - such as going to the bead store and making jewelry again after 20 years. Some interests were recent subjects - such as learning about the principles and mechanics of biofield Energy Medicine. I lost a sense of time on these artist dates and I felt much desired inspiration.

Intentionally cultivating joy led to a magical transformation in all aspects of my life. This metamorphosis inspired me to begin creating the guide you now hold in your hands. At the onset, I thought this book would simply be a joy journal. As I began writing, I realized sharing more of my journey and the other whole-health concepts in my personal and professional toolbox would create a deeper connection and make the book more powerful.

Flourish, A 365-Day Path Towards Love shows you a path to live wholeheartedly, remain light-filled, and be faithfully optimistic. These are steps I took, and continue to take, to return to my center naturally. The concepts are shared to help you flourish, *no matter where you are on your journey.* A forewarning: following joy, living with intention, and being true to yourself involves change and letting go. Despite the discomfort that comes with personal growth, the process consistently yields life force, wonder, and magic. And one more note before we begin, I urge you to modify my outlined methods as needed to create *your* personal highest and best healing route.

To receive a specially curated monthly newsletter to support your *Flourish* journey, subscribe at my website https://www.flourishintegralhealth.com/flourish.

This path provides a constant evolution and continues to reveal treasures, enlightening perspectives, and wonderful opportunities.

THE ELEMENTS OF FLOURISH

The Why and How of

The Flourish Integral Health logo is an ancient symbol of alchemy. It is placed as a watermark in the goals section of the workbook pages to help you transform your intentions into reality. From an energetic perspective, symbols, such as a Christian cross, are a conscious representation of the desired energy. They are used to communicate with a higher power. [4]

From here forward, I use the phrase God/the Universe to capture your word for a higher power be it God, Universe, Source, Higher Self, Spirit, The Big Guy Up There, or other name. My intention for this book is spiritual, not affiliation to a particular religion or spiritual tradition.

The Why and How of

I am passing along to you a most uplifting compliment received from a woodsman in the woods. *Where you walk the flowers bloom.* That is the essence I hope you feel as you walk this journey on a light-filled path in a magical forest towards your heart. Your presence fertilizes the soil of your soul as you transform and cultivate your inner fortitude and beauty.

A flower...is never just...a flower, but a resource for the exploration of color possibilities, of the evanescence of light and movement, the study of form and structure.

- PENELOPE LIVELY

{ finds joy in writing }

When your energies are brought into harmony, your body flourishes, your soul has a soil in which it can blossom.

- DONNA EDEN

{ finds joy in Energy Medicine }

The drive toward joy is the drive toward life.

- INGRID FETELL LEE

{ finds joy in the aesthetics of joy }

The Why and How of *Joy*

At the start of *Project Joy*, my aim was to understand all the intangible elements of joy and to be able to uncover more love inside myself. Ultimately, I wanted to share my findings to help everyone collectively live with more joy. I approached learning about joy as I believed a researcher would and aspired to decipher joy like noted researcher Brené Brown deciphers shame. I have a Bachelor's degree in engineering, so I put on my scientific hat and put my whole heart and soul into the exploration. Each day I noted my joy moments, along with several details: what sparked the feeling, what it felt like, what it looked like, and the time of day. Then, I took my observations and graphed daily joy moments to analyze if they were more frequently a result of a planned or spontaneous happening, and if the sense of joy was a product of an event or a specific thought. I considered the influence of sunshine on a day's joy, and reviewed if joy involved spending money. I also was mindful of the correlation between my overall emotional state and a day's particular number of joyful moments. To supplement my work, I read many articles and books about joy. I was so passionate about this experiment that I even contemplated creating a joy meter to help quantify the feeling (true!). My intention was to find a pattern, a formula for joy: to discover how to live responsibly and experience the most joy possible.

THE ELEMENTS OF JOY

Joy:
1. (noun) a feeling of great pleasure and happiness.
2. (verb) rejoice.

- OXFORD DICTIONARY

Joy is a spark of great delight that is felt deeply in your soul. Joy lights you up, and for the moments you are connected to the magic, you are elevated and feel completely whole.

The impalpable energy of joy exists in us and all around us, encompassing every aspect of our senses. The list of attributes is unlimited and unique to each person. Here is a start: I found, and you might too, that joy feels like warmth, confidence, support, encouragement, protection, release, possibility, and discovery. • Joy can also feel like your favorite pair of jeans, a cashmere sweater, or a loving embrace. • Joy looks like beauty, clarity, hope, thoughtfulness, diversity, and humanity. • Joy can also look like the faces of loved ones, a bouquet of bright balloons, a field of vibrant flowers, a walk in the sunshine, a front yard full of holiday lights, a text message from someone who cares about you, an adorable trick-or-treater's Halloween costume at your doorstep, a beautiful evening sunset, or discovering a long lost personal item. • Joy tastes rich. • Joy can also taste like a favorite meal, popcorn with a movie, s'mores over a campfire, the first sip of a morning beverage, or buttercream icing on a birthday cake. • Joy sounds magnificent. • Joy can also sound like music, laughter, recognition, a heartfelt eulogy, a thunderstorm, a motivational speech, or a healthy report from your doctor. • Joy smells bountiful. • Joy can also smell like sweet vanilla, fresh rain, cookies baking in the oven, or soup simmering on the stove in the cold of winter. Joy is truly luminous, sensational, and boundless.

Joy is a meeting place of deep intentionality, and self-forgetting, the bodily alchemy of what lies inside us in communion with what formally seemed outside, but is now neither, but becomes a voice between us and the world.

- DAVID WHYTE
{ finds joy in poetry }

MORE ON JOY

- Sparks of joy are frequently spontaneous. Countless moments of joy can be planned too.

- Joy is dependent on a connection to people, places, things, experiences, or memories. Catalysts for connection include loved ones, shining brightly for someone, nature, your home, a favorite vacation place, the open road, traditions, meaningful actions, and doing what you love.

- Joy happens at all moments of the day.

- Joy is found in being present, releasing control, observing, listening, allowing, creating, vulnerability, intimacy, courage, perseverance, movement, exploring, learning, growing, following your intuition, and being aware of your own personal joy.

- Sunshine is a joy booster, but a rainy day is full of joy too.

- Joy is not expensive. Joy is mostly priceless.

THINKING THIS SURE IS A LOT OF JOY?
THE POINT IS THAT JOY IS ALL OVER THE PLACE!

THE DIFFERENCE BETWEEN JOY AND HAPPINESS

The energy of joy is a higher vibration than happiness. Happiness is an emotional state relating to the overall contentment of life, whereas joy is a magical, divine feeling that is experienced in the present moment. Happiness is the result of external experiences, joy is based on an internal connection. Unlike happiness, joy can share space with other emotions. You can be grieving with your whole heart and still find a moment of joy. This is possible because joy is your true nature.

Joy seems to me a step beyond happiness — happiness is a sort of atmosphere you can live in sometimes, when you're lucky. Joy is a light that fills you with hope and faith and love.

- ADELA ROGERS ST. JOHNS
{ found joy in screenplays }

JOY SUPPORTS YOUR WHOLE HEALTH

Joy is the hum of Oneness. ...Joy is the barometer that lets us know everything is well tuned.

- MARK NEPO

{ finds joy in poetry }

Considering joy's full service for your whole health is an enlightening perspective.

Joy aids your physical health. Numerous medical studies report on the positive effects of elevated emotional states. In the *Time* article, "Health: the Biology of Joy," research by The University of Wisconsin (known as the "king of happiness research") along with research from Harvard's School of Public Health, The University of California, Berkeley, and Duke University indicates feelings like happiness and joy reduce the risk or limit the gravity of several health issues. Health issues positively influenced by joy include cardiovascular disease, diabetes, hypertension, and upper-respiratory infections. Studies show that experiencing joy also increases the development of antibodies and boosts the immune system. [5]

Joy supports your emotional health. If you struggle with emotions such as anxiety, depression, or shame, following joy will help lift your spirit and direct you toward contentment, feeling worthy of connection, and self-acceptance. Understanding joy also boosts your fortitude and self-reliance. Joy helps you remain faithful to yourself. Becoming more aware of joy helps you better trust yourself and the process of life. Joy empowers you to author your precious life.

Joy improves your mental health. When you find the key to your joy, you gain access to a life-long supply of positive change, inspiration, and hope. Understanding your joy allows you to more easily shift away from your discouraging voice. You become more confident in your decisions and yourself, optimistic, and truthful. You can process your thoughts constructively and make plans to relish with those people, places, things, and experiences that fulfill you. In darker moments, you can reflect on past joys and trust that more joyful moments are just ahead. You understand in a more meaningful way that joy will keep showing up because you have true affirmation it is woven into us and surrounds us.

Joy is a pillar for your spiritual well-being. Gaining insight into your joy helps strengthen your intuition and provides you with a deeper sense of your purpose. When you uncover bright gifts inside you that inspire yourself and others, you remain more authentic, heart-centered, and trusting in God/the Universe. You can see yourself and your path more clearly, and connect to your true essence at a deeper level.

THE KEY TO JOY

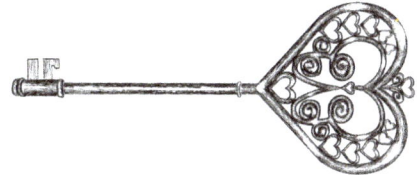

*Follow your bliss and the Universe will open doors
where there were only walls.*

- JOSEPH CAMPBELL

{ found joy in studying the human experience }

The key to inviting the most joy possible into your life is recognizing, understanding, and following your personal joy. How do you do that? This brings us to the first tool and practice for the *Flourish* journey: daily joy mindfulness journaling and joy dates.

Pay close attention to your joy each day. Notice how it is created and then honor the energy by writing about it. I find, and you might too, that the act of writing cultivates awareness. You most likely will experience a heightened sense of abundance, strength, and guidance. Take heed of the messages and follow your heart to discover more joy. Over time you will create a large, resourceful library of what brings you joy. Your joy library is located on page 286. Take a moment to flip there.

I also propose you make a commitment to take yourself on a weekly joy date. This dedicated joy seeking time is with you, and only you, to explore activities of interest and intrigue. Even if time feels limited, I encourage you to make this weekly commitment to yourself. The idea of a date with yourself might feel silly, or you might feel like you are not worthy. Keep going on dates with yourself, even if it is just for an hour a week. You are the star of your journey and deserve to take time for yourself to explore joy. If you are at a loss of where to venture, start by thinking about activities you loved as a child, or visit a bookstore, and see what peaks your interest. Approach your dates with curiosity. If your adventure feels frivolous, excellent! Joy is frivolous. Part of discovering more joy in your life involves allowing yourself time to tap further into your creativity and uncover interests and gifts that you may have lost sight of, only glimpsed, or have yet to discover. Be conscious of joy, and use this time to better understand and expand on the sensation. Know that the experience is supporting you. Allow yourself to be guided.

52 WEEKS OF JOY JOURNALING PAGES

There are 52 weeks of joy journal pages to support your daily mindfulness. Four weeks of joy journal pages are included in each monthly chapter. You will find an extra week in Month 1, 4, 7, and 10 (to total 52).

Be sure to note that each week begins with a simple 'act of kindness' suggestion to cultivate joy. Ideas rotate between extending kindness to yourself, and the people around you. When you extend compassion towards yourself or others, you are in the present moment, and you are able to more easily reach the frequency of joy.

There is space for you to write about your joy each day of the week and to detail your joy date. Take time before you go to bed, or the following morning, to reflect upon and write about your moments of joy. If you miss a few days, try to recall the previous day's highlights. Photos on your phone can help trigger moments you might have found joyful. Frequently photographing your joy helps too! Questions are offered to inspire reflection and personal growth at the end of each week. Thoughtfully complete the journal prompts, and plan for more joy. For example:

Sunday ___9/24___ I found a scene for a future painting while on my joy date. It felt inspiring. I happened upon an adorable roadside farmer's stand and purchased beautiful Gladiolus stem flowers. I ate a delicious sandwich and treated myself to a bag of heavenly potato chips in the sunshine. I had a heart-filling conversation with a friend. I used Washi tape for the first time in my journal. All joy!

In this example, by being mindful of joy, in addition to the present moment joy, I have a painting project to look forward to, a new destination for flowers and lunch, a memory of a bright conversation, and a fun journaling tool. I will draw upon each to lift my spirit.

I suggest using three book darts or page markers for the journey, one to locate your place on the joy journal pages, one to mark your joy library, and one to find your place on the monthly intentional pages (introduced in the next chapter). Book darts are a great way to mark your place in a book and they don't crease your page like a paper clip.

The time commitment for the joy journaling is about five minutes per day, and 15 additional minutes weekly for reflection and planning.

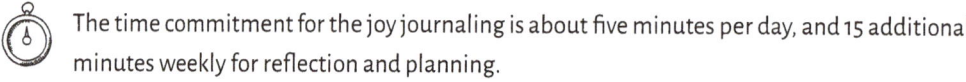

On this path you will learn all about your personal joy, discover a host of gifts within and around yourself, and gain a deeper sense of purpose. The journey will reveal synchronicities and miracles. *Joy is beautifully simple. Joy is a lifeline. Joy is the journey.*

Your Initial Thoughts on Joy

1. At the onset of this journey, note what you believe creates joy in your life.

2. Recall activities you have enjoyed in the past, but have put aside.

3. Are there classes, skills, or a hobby you have wanted to explore, but have yet to?

4. What inspires you?

For the raindrop, joy is entering the lake.

- GHALIB

{ found joy in poetry }

Our intention creates our reality.

- WAYNE DYER

{ found joy in personal empowerment }

The Why and How of

Intention

Like joy, intention is an intangible energy that is found within and around us. Intention can be thought of as a goal. The aim is linked within your mind, body, and spirit, and it is the energy of intention that influences every aspect of your life. Your intentions ripple beyond yourself.

It is because intentions are so powerful that they are another foundational element of the *Flourish* journey. While I was pursuing a practitioner certification in Energy Medicine through the Healing Touch Program, I learned the importance of setting intentions. Every Healing Touch energy session begins with an intention statement defining what health issue a client wants to reduce, or release, and their indicated outcome. A pain scale is utilized to measure the health goal before and after each session. The left brain in me appreciates this measuring aspect because it gives validity to a mysterious way of working. I noticed that setting intentions impacted the overall effectiveness of a healing session, and I was amazed at how a positive shift consistently took place. I began to actively set intentions throughout my life. From a healing perspective, it is clear that pausing to reflect upon your desires and set an intention for an experience, influences the future.

THE ELEMENTS OF INTENTION

Intention:
1. (noun) a thing intended; an aim or plan.
2. (noun) *Medicine*, the healing process of a wound.

- OXFORD DICTIONARY

If we are here to heal, intention in its most simplistic form, as defined by Oxford Dictionary, could be interpreted as the medicine for our wounds. Similar to setting a broken bone to heal a fracture, setting intentions is an act of healing. I believe we set intentions to manifest our tangible creative pursuits and desires. At the same time, we can focus inward to heal fragmented parts of ourselves that are interconnected to our outward goals. Examining your intentions reveals what you are wholly seeking.

Energy cannot be created or destroyed, it can only be changed from one form to another.

- ALBERT EINSTEIN

{ found joy in physics }

The First Law of Thermodynamics states that energy is always conserved. It cannot be created or destroyed. As you approach your intentions with this scientific lens, consider that you are reducing, or releasing, an undesired energy and converting it into energy that elevates your spirit. An example of this alchemy is when you are angry or feel a tinge of envy, and you harness that feeling to fuel positive change in your life. You can repurpose darkness to make light. Extra momentum is gained towards your goals with this self-healing perspective in mind.

INTENTIONS SUPPORT YOUR WHOLE HEALTH

Intention leads to behaviors which leads to habits which lead to personality development which leads to destiny.

- JACK KORNFIELD

{ finds joy in Buddhism }

If you find this introduction to setting whole health intentions feels dry, please remain open! It is brief and integral to the journey. The core concept is revisited in bright detail in Month No. 1.

Intention aids your physical health. Any aspect of your physical health you desire to change can be treated by setting an intention statement. For example, if you want to lose weight, I invite you to survey what it is that you need to release to lose weight and why. You could say that reducing caloric intake would help achieve that desire. From a healing perspective, I suggest looking deeper. When do you find yourself overeating? You might eat when you are anxious. Next, lovingly look at the reason why you want to lose weight. You might want to lose weight so your clothing fits more comfortably -- comfort is the keyword. An intention statement could be: I release anxiety as evidenced by losing five to ten pounds. At the root, your focus, and desired alchemy energy conversion is turning anxious energy into feeling comfortable. Subsequently, your work is about listening to your heart and making the necessary changes to feel less anxiety and more comfort.

Intention supports your emotional health. To build on the example above, in the case of your emotional health, you might want to feel happier. What do you want to release? If you want to release something fear-based, your intention statement could read: I release fear as evidenced by feeling happier. Your deeper work is to survey what you are afraid of; maybe you're afraid of failure. Fear of failure is what holds you back from realizing your dreams. Your focus is on turning the energy of fear of failure into heartfelt success. A compassionate suggestion is to look at all the areas of your life where you feel successful.

Intention improves your mental health. Your intention could be that you would like to worry less. First, think about what you are worried about. Maybe you're worried about your finances. You drill down further and realize that you really would like to purchase a new home. The next question to ask yourself is: what do you want to feel instead of feeling worried? You want to feel secure. The intention statement might read something like this: I release worry as evidenced by purchasing a new home. At the root, your focus is on gaining a feeling of security. Your inner work is about making shifts to worry less and feel secure as you go about the process of purchasing a home. Here, too, I'm illustrating the power of looking within and making the changes required to achieve your full desires.

Intention is a pillar for your spiritual well-being. What do you want more of on a spiritual level? Let's say you answer, faith. What do you need to release to grow more in faith? If your answer is control, the statement could read like this: I release control as evidenced by feeling more faithful. Your focus is on releasing your desire for control and gaining faith in God/the Universe (I believe this is cultivating love!) To manifest your desire, you could release control, and observe what materializes. You might support your growth process by noting all the joyfully supportive surprises in your life each day.

THE KEY TO INTENTION

And every day, the world will drag you by the hand, yelling, "This is important! And this is important! And this is important! You need to worry about this! And this! And this!" And each day it is up to you to yank your hand back, put it on your heart and say, "No. This is what's important."

- IAIN THOMAS

{ finds joy in poetry }

I find, and you might too, that in the busyness of life, it can be challenging to find silence to gain clarity about your values and true desires. This is a big part of the "why" behind this guidebook. It is a supportive framework for identifying and then bringing to life your deepest desires. *Flourish* is a creative vehicle to help you focus your energy on what you want the most in life! This brings us to the second key for the journey: routine focus on your meaningful intentions.

12 MONTHS OF INTENTION JOURNALING PAGES

There are 12 months of intention journal spreads (one in each chapter). Month No. 1 includes an exercise to identify your heart's desires and discover the necessary energy transformations for you to feel complete. The intentional journaling tool helps you concentrate on your desired goals and observe your healing practices. Taking dedicated steps, no matter how small, in the direction of your dreams routinely, creates significant change on your path. The centered attention accumulates and, one day, you arrive at your destination. Take heart that your particular aim may not always materialize exactly as you planned. This is part of the magical mystery of life!

In the morning spend a few mindful moments reflecting on your intentions. Consider the next step for your tangible goal, and visualize the energy transformation. Then, in the evening, or following morning, record the time spent towards your desires and consider your energy gains. I encourage you to make notes indexing both your efforts towards your desired goal and your alchemy (remember the First Law of Thermodynamics). How you mark up the tracker is personal preference. You might want to add checkmarks, or if you are measuring something like your weight, miles biked, or minutes meditating, you can write that number. You could also create a key and shade the boxes in different colors if you are a visual learner. You might not intend to work towards each intention every day of the month. If that is the case, you could shade or color those squares as dedicated free days. You can also pencil in the days of the week at the top of each grid. If you like to tally, or sum, there is a blank space at the end of each monthly grid to do so. Feel free to get creative with the sheet and make it work for you! You will be so joyfully surprised about the results of your heartfelt dedication. Here are some examples:

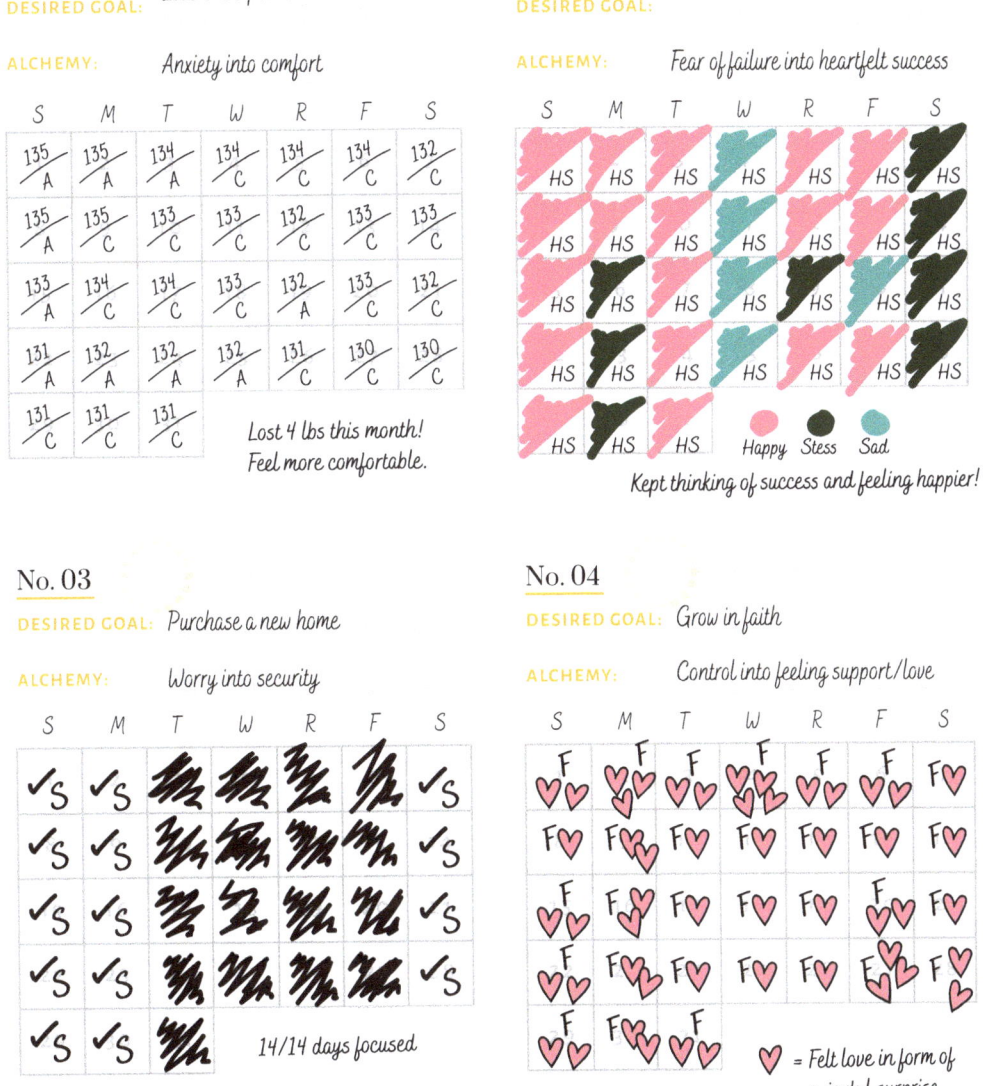

No. 01

DESIRED GOAL: *Lose 5-10 pounds*

ALCHEMY: *Anxiety into comfort*

S	M	T	W	R	F	S
135/A	135/A	134/A	134/C	134/C	134/C	132/C
135/A	135/C	133/C	133/C	132/C	133/C	133/C
133/A	134/C	134/C	133/C	132/A	133/C	132/C
131/A	132/A	132/A	132/A	131/C	130/C	130/C
131/C	131/C	131/C				

Lost 4 lbs this month! Feel more comfortable.

No. 02

DESIRED GOAL: *Feel happier*

ALCHEMY: *Fear of failure into heartfelt success*

Happy · Stess · Sad

Kept thinking of success and feeling happier!

No. 03

DESIRED GOAL: *Purchase a new home*

ALCHEMY: *Worry into security*

14/14 days focused

= dedicated free day

No. 04

DESIRED GOAL: *Grow in faith*

ALCHEMY: *Control into feeling support/love*

♡ = Felt love in form of a joyful surprise. Faith grew!

Questions are offered to inspire reflection at the end of each month, inviting you to consider how you spent your time and your progress towards your goals. This page includes space to consider resistance, bumps in the road, possible detours, and re-routing! The reflection is written to help you celebrate your achievements, and to contemplate any beneficial adjustments you might make. This study will make certain that you are navigating from your heart-center as you move towards your whole destination.

 The time commitment for the intention journaling is about 15 minutes per day and 30 additional minutes monthly for reflection and planning.

Setting intentions has a profound influence on your transformation to achieve your true desires.

Often people attempt to live their lives backwards: they try to have more things, or more money, in order to do more of what they want so that they will be happier. The way it actually works is the reverse. You must first be who you really are, then, do what you need to do, in order to have what you really want.

- MARGARET YOUNG

{ finds joy in writing }

THE ELEMENTS OF INTENTIONAL COLOR

The Why and How of

Our energy bodies include seven main energy centers called chakras. Chakra is the Sanskrit word for wheel, or circle. The spinning wheels run vertically up your spine and create your individual energy field that supports your physical, emotional, mental, and spiritual being. The first chakra is located at the base of the spine. The seventh chakra is around the crown of your head. These two chakras expand towards the Earth and the Universe, respectively. The other five chakras expand in front of, and behind you. Each chakra center has attributes that inform your being including a purpose, focus, "I" statement, and color.

On the *Flourish* journey, the page accent hues are representative of the chakra that corresponds to the focus of the month's intentions. You will also find a colorful place to write your own "I" statements each month. "I" statements are assertions about yourself and your beliefs that support self-awareness. These statements empower you by capturing how you feel and clarifying what you need, or want. It is important to honor your feelings because your emotions can help to guide you. When writing "I" statements about the future, be sure to write in the positive tense.

Color is a power which directly influences the soul.

- WASSILY KANDINSKY

{ found joy in painting }

Life is a train of moods like a string of beads, and
as we pass through them, they prove to be many
colored lenses which paint the world their own hue,
and each shows only what lies in its focus.

- RALPH WALDO EMERSON

{ found joy in writing }

WHERE JOY AND INTENTION MEET IS MAGICAL

We are at our very best, and we are happiest, when we are fully engaged in work we enjoy on the journey toward the goal we've established for ourselves. It gives meaning to our time off and comfort to our sleep. It makes everything else in life so wonderful, so worthwhile.

- EARL NIGHTINGALE

{ found joy in meaningful existence }

Joy flourishes in an atmosphere of intentional growth, especially when you are working towards your deepest desires. One of the first books I read, when I began to immerse myself in the study of joy, was Gretchen Rubin's *New York Times* bestseller *The Happiness Project*. Throughout the book, Gretchen chronicles her year-long experiment conducted to discover the path to true happiness. Gretchen found that it was the actual pursuit of a goal that provided the utmost happiness.[6] To further illustrate, in the article, "Health: the Biology of Joy" mentioned earlier, researchers indicate that moving towards a goal increases levels of your body's chemical messenger dopamine. Dopamine is a neurotransmitter that is linked to how we feel pleasure. My research, too, affirms that working towards a goal often creates more joy than the actual completion of the goal itself. While spending time on your pursuit, you are in the present moment where the most peace, love, and pure joy are felt.

You hold the keys of joy and intention. *Magic resides in this union. Magic lives in your dreams that are in flight.*

And above all, watch with glittering eyes the whole world around you because the greatest secrets are always hidden in the most unlikely places. Those who don't believe in magic will never find it.

- ROALD DAHL

{ found joy in writing }

Love

Eternity

Water Rest Area

Picnic Rest Area

Vista Rest Area

Month No. 1

Setting Your Intentions

What is my calling, my life's aim?
What inspires me the most? What activity or service is
my core values urging me to pursue?

- STEVEN COVEY

{ found joy in principle centered living }

The journey begins!

Imagine you are on the 365-day path. The keys of joy and intention are attached to your travel bag. You are ready to explore the forest and make choices in support of growing in love. Perhaps you feel some trepidation towards the unknown but you mostly feel excited, curious, and hopeful.

You have walked from the trailhead, parallel to the River of Dreams, and have arrived at lantern No.1. You set down your travel bag at this first rest stop, and sit down on a welcoming tree stump. You close your eyes and listen to the flow of the rolling, meditative, water. You begin to see yourself as a beautiful butterfly just taking flight for the first time from your cocoon. With wings stretched wide, you are ready to glide towards freedom. Where are you going? Imagine limitless possibility.

Intentional living is the bridge to significance. At the end of every year I take time out to reflect and evaluate the events of the previous year - what went well and what needed improvement. From that inventory, I lay out my next year - how I intend to live, make the best use of my time and maximize adding value to others. Success asks, "How can I add value to myself? Significance asks, "How can I add value to others? It is your intention that leads itself to significance.

- JOHN C. MAXWELL

{ finds joy in leadership }

Muladhara is the first chakra. It is also known as your root chakra. Located at the base of your spine, it is red and represents your physical body, physical health, sense of safety, security, and your foundation. A root chakra "I" statement is, "I am here". This month you will connect to your root center to build your base for the journey.

Welcome to Month No. 1 of the *Flourish* journey. Before you start engaging with the material in each chapter, go to a quiet place, take a few settling deep breaths, and find a comfortable space within yourself. Shift to your peaceful center so you can receive your inner guidance. I propose you take each step of the path at your own pace.

The first month's exercises create the foundation for the adventure. These pages are dedicated to helping you translate your love-based wishes, first onto paper, and then into reality. This inner voyage is designed to inspire you, help you find clarity, instill courage, and support your success. I also encourage you to see change and the unknown as opportunity.

PREPARING FOR THE JOURNEY

Below are two reflection exercises to prepare you for setting your intentions.

1. RELEASING THE PAST

Before deciding what you will create, take some time to reflect on what you would like to release. Consider what holds you back from achieving your dreams. Part of the process of moving forward is letting go. Imagine you are a traveler and currently at customs, what are the items you would pull out of your travel bag and leave behind before heading on your journey?

What would you like to release?

What are lessons learned from what you are releasing?

Take a deep breath and as you exhale, imagine releasing what you no longer want to carry from your whole being; intend to convert it into positive energy to support you.

2. HONORING THE PAST

Now think about past successes. Recall the moments you have proudly crossed the finish line you set for yourself. Remember the times in your life where you felt full of elevating love. Past highs are radiant reminders that you can achieve what you are setting forth to accomplish now. Take time to honor yourself and your dedication to your realized dreams.

What are your greatest accomplishments and successes?

How did you achieve them? What were the secrets to your success?

What have been your biggest surprises or insights on those journeys?

SETTING YOUR INTENTIONS

Nothing happens unless we dream first.

- CARL SANDBURG

{ found joy in poetry }

Throughout this journey, it is important to keep your heart and mind wide open. While you create your intentions, imagine that God/the Universe will deliver all you desire.

1. VIEW THE FACETS OF YOU

As you begin, I encourage you to consider yourself as a physical, emotional, mental, and spiritual being. View each facet of yourself as connected; movement in one area will affect the whole you. Now, think about your health, home, relationships, career, education, finances, community, spirituality, and leisure.

2. DEFINE YOUR GOALS

With compassion, survey your heart's desires and decide what your goals are. What do you want to manifest in your life? Dream big!

Do you have physical or mental health goals?

Are there relationships you would like to foster?

Do you have home improvement plans?

Do you have a career related dream?

What are your financial goals?

Is there a new exercise habit you would like to create?

Would you like to become more involved in your community?

Are there classes you would like to take?

Would you like to gain clarity on your spiritual beliefs?

3. CONSIDER WHY THIS IS IMPORTANT TO YOU

To help clarify your true aspirations, I invite you to consider two whys. Why you are setting the aim? & Why it is important to you? Your heart is the fuel for your transformation, so your intentions need to be meaningful. Ultimately, the goal needs to be for *you*. Your goal might be in service to others, but be sure you desire it from a place of love, rather than fear.

4. INSPECT WHAT YOU NEED TO RELEASE

It is important to consider what needs to be released in order to realize your dreams. Remember, you can convert the energy of what you release (->) to create your desires. You will most likely find that what you want to let go of appears in several aspects of your life. Releasing it in one area helps diminish its influence in others. (You might have just left it at customs!) If you enjoy numerical-tracking, you could imagine placing what you want to shed on the airport baggage scale and assign a weight to it. On a scale of 1-10, ten being the heaviest, what does it weigh? Noting its unit of measure, allows you an opportunity to reflect back over time and see your growth in its release. (Very heavy baggage has great potential for brilliance!)

5. CREATE YOUR INTENTION STATEMENT

To feel clear, empowered, and supported, I encourage you to write a full intention statement for each of your aims in the format: I reduce, or release {insert what you are letting go} as evidenced by {insert your goal}. This is a supportive healing statement in a format used by the Healing Touch Program®. The purpose of an intention statement is to direct your energy towards your whole desires. Repeat your written intention, aloud or to yourself, until it feels part of you.

6. BE CLEAR ABOUT THE ENERGY YOU WANT TO GAIN

When you release the energy of what you no longer want (#4), you can visualize your holistic health aspirations more clearly. Reflect on the positive attribute you desire. In place of feeling #4, what do you want to feel, or gain?

7. IDENTIFY YOUR ALCHEMY

Identify the energy that you will transform from dark to light as you expand into your full potential. This is your opportunity to turn an undesirable fear, or pain, into gold. Your inner work is to change #4 into #6. To do this, keep focusing your healing thoughts towards (->) #6. Continue to imagine that you are already at your destination. Envision your end goal as though it has already been realized.

The secret of change is to focus all of your energy not on fighting the old, but on building the new.

- SOCRATES

{ found joy in philosophy }

Below are a few personal examples to illustrate the sequence. You will find an open section for you to write your own foundational statements for the journey on the next page. Please be patient with yourself as you work through what arises in your heart and mind. Translating your inner terrain to paper is not always easy, but it is well worth the effort. The more clear you are, the easier it is to make your dreams reality.

EXAMPLE NO. 1

1. FACET OF YOU: *Career*

2. DESIRED GOAL: *I would like to create a successful personal growth journal.*

3. WHY SETTING & WHY IMPORTANT: *To help people experience more joy, live with more intention, and be true to themselves. This is important because I feel it is part of my creative healing process.*

4. WHAT YOU NEED TO RELEASE (WEIGHT): *Self-doubt (9 is the weight)*

5. FULL HEALING INTENTION STATEMENT: *I release {insert what you are letting go} as evidenced by {insert your goal}: I release self-doubt as evidenced by creating a successful personal growth journal.*

6. ENERGY GAIN FOR WHOLENESS: *My focus is on gaining heartfelt confidence.*

7. ALCHEMY: *Self-doubt into (->) heartfelt confidence (HC).*

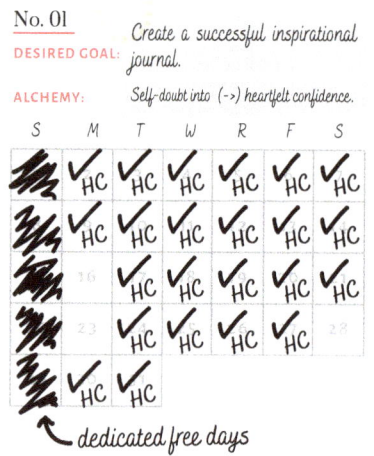

No. 01
DESIRED GOAL: *Create a successful inspirational journal.*

ALCHEMY: *Self-doubt into (->) heartfelt confidence.*

dedicated free days

{ In this example, my aim is to create the journal daily and to gain heartfelt confidence (HC). By using this tracker, I will hold myself accountable to my goal, in addition to observing if my overall sense of heartfelt confidence increases over time. This completed tracker illustrates this month I worked almost everyday as planned. Each time I worked on the journal, I gained heartfelt confidence. }

1. FACET OF YOU: *Health*

2. DESIRED GOAL: *I would like to meditate daily for 15 minutes.*

3. WHY SETTING & WHY IMPORTANT: *To feel centered and better attuned to God/the Universe. This is important because it will help me gain clarity.*

4. WHAT YOU NEED TO RELEASE (WEIGHT): *Fear based feeling that I don't have enough time. (7 is the weight)*

5. FULL HEALING INTENTION STATEMENT: *I release {insert what you are letting go} as evidenced by {insert your goal}:I release a recurring fearful feeling that I don't have enough time as evidenced by meditating daily for 15 minutes.*

6. ENERGY GAIN FOR WHOLENESS: *My focus is on gaining clarity.*

7. ALCHEMY: *Rushed fearful feeling into (->) clarity (C).*

No. 02
DESIRED GOAL: *Meditate for 15 min.*

ALCHEMY: *Rush fearful feeling into (->) clarity.*

S	M	T	W	R	F	S
15/C	15/C	15/C	15/C	15/C	15/C	15/C
15/C	15/C	15/C	10/C	15/C	15/C	10/C
15/C	15/C	10/C	15/C	15/C	15/C	15/C
15/C	15/C	15/C	15/C	10/C	15/C	15/C
5/C	15/C	15/C				

{ In this example, my aim is to meditate for 15 minutes daily in an effort to gain clarity (C). By using this tracker, I will hold myself accountable to my daily meditation goal. I can also note insights on clarity gain through my practice. This completed tracker illustrates this month I meditated everyday; some days less than 15 minutes as planned. I gained clarity everyday except one. }

The future belongs to those who believe in the beauty of their dreams.

-ELEANOR ROOSEVELT

{ found joy in activism }

Your Intentions

1. Facet of You:

2. Desired Goal:

3. Why Setting & Why Important :

4. What You Need to Release (Weight):

5. Full Healing Intention Statement: I release {insert what you are letting go} as evidenced by {insert your goal}:

6. Energy Gain for Wholeness:

7. Alchemy:

---

1. Facet of You:

2. Desired Goal:

3. Why Setting & Why Important :

4. What You Need to Release (Weight):

5. Full Healing Intention Statement: I release {insert what you are letting go} as evidenced by {insert your goal}:

6. Energy Gain for Wholeness:

7. Alchemy:

---

1. Facet of You:

2. Desired Goal:

3. Why Setting & Why Important :

4. What You Need to Release (Weight):

5. Full Healing Intention Statement: I release {insert what you are letting go} as evidenced by {insert your goal}:

6. Energy Gain for Wholeness:

7. Alchemy:

1. Facet of You:

2. Desired Goal:

3. Why Setting & Why Important :

4. What You Need to Release (Weight):

5. Full Healing Intention Statement: I release {insert what you are letting go} as evidenced by {insert your goal}:

6. Energy Gain for Wholeness:

7. Alchemy:

---

1. Facet of You:

2. Desired Goal:

3. Why Setting & Why Important :

4. What You Need to Release (Weight):

5. Full Healing Intention Statement: I release {insert what you are letting go} as evidenced by {insert your goal}:

6. Energy Gain for Wholeness:

7. Alchemy:

---

1. Facet of You:

2. Desired Goal:

3. Why Setting & Why Important :

4. What You Need to Release (Weight):

5. Full Healing Intention Statement: I release {insert what you are letting go} as evidenced by {insert your goal}:

6. Energy Gain for Wholeness:

7. Alchemy:

Your Keyword for the Journey

Here is one more exercise to gain inner strength for the process. A keyword helps keep you centered and focused on what you want to experience. It's a positive energy to hold before you start your day. You'll reflect on this keyword regularly and draw a feeling of empowerment from it as you progress.

Focus inward and concentrate on your breath. Feel your stomach expand with each inhalation and contract with each exhalation. Set the intention to find the keyword that will best help you flourish for the next 12 months.

Think about the energy above you and reach for the furthest part of the skies. From that place imagine a sprinkling of sparkling light filtering into the crown of your head. Breathe in the bright, celestial light. Now, imagine the light running down through your body, filling your heart, and reaching to the bottoms of your feet. When the light reaches the soles of your feet, begin to ground yourself. Imagine your legs extending beyond your body and sinking deep down into the core of the Earth. Continue focusing on your breath and see your toes slide into the core.

When you are ready, slowly bring your awareness back to your heart center and imagine a large ball of healing white light residing there. Ask to sense the word that will best help support your growth. The first word that arrives is most likely your keyword. Trust the process.

What is your keyword?

How does that word make you feel?

How does it relate to your intentions?

Equipped with the foundational tools for the journey, you are on your way to realizing your desires. The next step is transferring your keyword and the focus of your intentions onto the first monthly tracker located on page 60. Start with a comfortable number of goals. Review your list, and select the first three or four intentions that seem the most pressing to you. As you solidify your habits and manifest, some intentions drop off the tracker, and you can introduce new ones from your list. Now is a great time to start journaling about your joy too! (located on page 50)

Enjoy the journey towards fulfilling your true potential.

In the Universe there is an immeasurable, indescribable force which shamans call intent, and absolutely everything that exists in the entire cosmos is attached to intent by a connecting link.

- CARLOS CASTANEDA

{ found joy in anthropology }

Week No. 1 *Your Joy*

Cultivate joy! | Follow your intuition!

Record moments of joy each day

What was your joy? Who/What gave rise to the joy? What did it feel, look, taste, smell, or sound like?

The process of reflective writing supports awareness. Awareness of what brings you joy serves as a heart-centered, resourceful compass, and unfolds more joy. The key to the journey is recognizing, understanding, and following -- your personal joy.

Joy Date · Write about your joy date - what you explored and how you felt.

Sunday _____

Monday _____

Tuesday _____

Wednesday _____

Thursday _____

Friday _____

Saturday _____

Week In Review

What was your most joyful moment this week? What themes, new or already noted, did you find in your joy moments?

The subjects have a wonderful story to tell you. And if you follow the essence -- more joy and purpose will come to light. Keep exploring your joy and add discoveries to your joy library.

Was any of your joy this week the product of working through fear and lessening your resistance towards a goal?

Recall scenarios where working through fear to reach a goal resulted in tremendous joy. With this awareness, in fearful moments you will find courage to move forward.

What were your achievements this week? Did you gain any new insights?

Note your most successful accomplishments, quality time with loved ones, and enlightening moments. Flip back periodically to honor your attentiveness to your priorities and review what you have learned.

Did you face challenges this week? Do you see different possibilities? How will you adjust moving forward?

Learning happens when you reflect and make adjustments to your course. Your growth is the product of working through struggles and finding a heart-centered solution. Joy resides here, too!

What kindness did you extend? How did you feel during and afterward?

Noting the kindness you extend during the week helps you to honor your light and love yourself more.

Use this space to begin planning for more joy in your life.

Dedicating time for joy makes your days brighter and more meaningful.

People

Places

Things

Experiences

Joy Date Ideas

Week No. 2 *Your Joy*

Cultivate joy!

Send someone a greeting card to let them know you are thinking of them!

Record moments of joy each day

What was your joy? Who/What gave rise to the joy? What did it feel, look, taste, smell, or sound like?

The process of reflective writing supports awareness. Awareness of what brings you joy serves as a heart-centered, resourceful compass, and unfolds more joy. The key to the journey is recognizing, understanding, and following -- your personal joy.

Joy Date · Write about your joy date - what you explored and how you felt.

Sunday _____

Monday _____

Tuesday _____

Wednesday _____

Thursday _____

Friday _____

Saturday _____

Week In Review

What was your most joyful moment this week? What themes, new or already noted, did you find in your joy moments?

The subjects have a wonderful story to tell you. And if you follow the essence -- more joy and purpose will come to light. Keep exploring your joy and add discoveries to your joy library.

No soul that seriously and constantly desires joy will ever miss it. Those who seek find. To those who knock it is opened.

- C.S. LEWIS

{ found joy in theology }

Was any of your joy this week the product of working through fear and lessening your resistance towards a goal?

Recall scenarios where working through fear to reach a goal resulted in tremendous joy. With this awareness, in fearful moments you will find courage to move forward.

What were your achievements this week? Did you gain any new insights?

Note your most successful accomplishments, quality time with loved ones, and enlightening moments. Flip back periodically to honor your attentiveness to your priorities and review what you have learned.

Did you face challenges this week? Do you see different possibilities? How will you adjust moving forward?

Learning happens when you reflect and make adjustments to your course. Your growth is the product of working through struggles and finding a heart-centered solution. Joy resides here, too!

What kindness did you extend? How did you feel during and afterward?

Noting the kindness you extend during the week helps you to honor your light and love yourself more.

Use this space to begin planning for more joy in your life.

Dedicating time for joy makes your days brighter and more meaningful.

People

Places

Things

Experiences

Joy Date Ideas

Week No. 3 *Your Joy*

Cultivate joy! | Spend time in nature, and explore somewhere new!

Record moments of joy each day | What was your joy? Who/What gave rise to the joy? What did it feel, look, taste, smell, or sound like?

The process of reflective writing supports awareness. Awareness of what brings you joy serves as a heart-centered, resourceful compass, and unfolds more joy. The key to the journey is recognizing, understanding, and following -- your personal joy.

Joy Date · Write about your joy date - what you explored and how you felt.

_____

Sunday _____

Monday _____

Tuesday _____

Wednesday _____

Thursday _____

Friday _____

Saturday _____

Week In Review

What was your most joyful moment this week? What themes, new or already noted, did you find in your joy moments?

The subjects have a wonderful story to tell you. And if you follow the essence -- more joy and purpose will come to light. Keep exploring your joy and add discoveries to your joy library.

Was any of your joy this week the product of working through fear and lessening your resistance towards a goal?

Recall scenarios where working through fear to reach a goal resulted in tremendous joy. With this awareness, in fearful moments you will find courage to move forward.

What were your achievements this week? Did you gain any new insights?

Note your most successful accomplishments, quality time with loved ones, and enlightening moments. Flip back periodically to honor your attentiveness to your priorities and review what you have learned.

Did you face challenges this week? Do you see different possibilities? How will you adjust moving forward?

Learning happens when you reflect and make adjustments to your course. Your growth is the product of working through struggles and finding a heart-centered solution. Joy resides here, too!

What kindness did you extend? How did you feel during and afterward?

Noting the kindness you extend during the week helps you to honor your light and love yourself more.

Use this space to begin planning for more joy in your life.

Dedicating time for joy makes your days brighter and more meaningful.

People

Places

Things

Experiences

Joy Date Ideas

Week No. 4 *Your Joy*

Cultivate joy! | Deliver flowers to a friend, to celebrate an occassion, or to express your gratitude!

Record moments of joy each day | What was your joy? Who/What gave rise to the joy? What did it feel, look, taste, smell, or sound like?

The process of reflective writing supports awareness. Awareness of what brings you joy serves as a heart-centered, resourceful compass, and unfolds more joy. The key to the journey is recognizing, understanding, and following -- your personal joy.

Joy Date · Write about your joy date - what you explored and how you felt.

_____

Sunday _____

_____

Monday _____

_____

Tuesday _____

_____

Wednesday _____

_____

Thursday _____

_____

Friday _____

_____

Saturday _____

_____

Week In Review

What was your most joyful moment this week? What themes, new or already noted, did you find in your joy moments?

The subjects have a wonderful story to tell you. And if you follow the essence -- more joy and purpose will come to light. Keep exploring your joy and add discoveries to your joy library.

Was any of your joy this week the product of working through fear and lessening your resistance towards a goal?

Recall scenarios where working through fear to reach a goal resulted in tremendous joy. With this awareness, in fearful moments you will find courage to move forward.

What were your achievements this week? Did you gain any new insights?

Note your most successful accomplishments, quality time with loved ones, and enlightening moments. Flip back periodically to honor your attentiveness to your priorities and review what you have learned.

Did you face challenges this week? Do you see different possibilities? How will you adjust moving forward?

Learning happens when you reflect and make adjustments to your course. Your growth is the product of working through struggles and finding a heart-centered solution. Joy resides here, too!

What kindness did you extend? How did you feel during and afterward?

Noting the kindness you extend during the week helps you to honor your light and love yourself more.

Use this space to begin planning for more joy in your life.

Dedicating time for joy makes your days brighter and more meaningful.

People

Places

Things

Experiences

Joy Date Ideas

Week No. 5   *Your Joy*

Cultivate joy! | Set a recurring kudos reminder on your phone, at a time of day that you need a lift!

Record moments of joy each day | What was your joy? Who/What gave rise to the joy? What did it feel, look, taste, smell, or sound like?

The process of reflective writing supports awareness. Awareness of what brings you joy serves as a heart-centered, resourceful compass, and unfolds more joy. The key to the journey is recognizing, understanding, and following -- your personal joy.

Joy Date · Write about your joy date - what you explored and how you felt.

_____

Sunday _____

_____

Monday _____

_____

Tuesday _____

_____

Wednesday _____

_____

Thursday _____

_____

Friday _____

_____

Saturday _____

_____

Week In Review

What was your most joyful moment this week? What themes, new or already noted, did you find in your joy moments?

The subjects have a wonderful story to tell you. And if you follow the essence -- more joy and purpose will come to light. Keep exploring your joy and add discoveries to your joy library.

Was any of your joy this week the product of working through fear and lessening your resistance towards a goal?

Recall scenarios where working through fear to reach a goal resulted in tremendous joy. With this awareness, in fearful moments you will find courage to move forward.

What were your achievements this week? Did you gain any new insights?

Note your most successful accomplishments, quality time with loved ones, and enlightening moments. Flip back periodically to honor your attentiveness to your priorities and review what you have learned.

Did you face challenges this week? Do you see different possibilities? How will you adjust moving forward?

Learning happens when you reflect and make adjustments to your course. Your growth is the product of working through struggles and finding a heart-centered solution. Joy resides here, too!

What kindness did you extend? How did you feel during and afterward?

Noting the kindness you extend during the week helps you to honor your light and love yourself more.

Use this space to begin planning for more joy in your life.

Dedicating time for joy makes your days brighter and more meaningful.

People

Places

Things

Experiences

Joy Date Ideas

Month No. 1 *Your Intentions*

YOUR KEYWORD

Along with your keyword, draw on the inner strength of curiosity, hope, and self-compassion as you approach your intentions.

Track the energy that you put towards your aspirations, and observe what is gained. Remember that being intentional about how you spend your time will help you achieve your goals. Where your attention goes, your energy flows.

No. 01

DESIRED GOAL:

ALCHEMY:

1	2	3	4	5	6	7
8	9	10	11	12	13	14
15	16	17	18	19	20	21
22	23	24	25	26	27	28
29	30	31				

No. 02

DESIRED GOAL:

ALCHEMY:

1	2	3	4	5	6	7
8	9	10	11	12	13	14
15	16	17	18	19	20	21
22	23	24	25	26	27	28
29	30	31				

No. 03

DESIRED GOAL:

ALCHEMY:

1	2	3	4	5	6	7
8	9	10	11	12	13	14
15	16	17	18	19	20	21
22	23	24	25	26	27	28
29	30	31				

No. 04

DESIRED GOAL:

ALCHEMY:

1	2	3	4	5	6	7
8	9	10	11	12	13	14
15	16	17	18	19	20	21
22	23	24	25	26	27	28
29	30	31				

Month In Review

Reflect on your time spent working towards your intentions.
Did you spend time as planned on your goals? Have you released what you needed to, and started to refine your focus? Record below a yes, partial, or no.

GOAL/ALCHEMY No. 01

GOAL/ALCHEMY No. 02

GOAL/ALCHEMY No. 03

GOAL/ALCHEMY No. 04

The yesses: Congratulations! Write about your successes.
How do you feel? What does this accomplishment offer you? If you no longer need to track this goal, consider introducing a new intention from your Month No. 1 exercise.

The partials: Is there anything new that you could implement that would help you achieve your goals?
Do you need to be more intentional in setting aside time for your desires? Do you need to break the goal down into smaller steps? Be kind to yourself as you process.

The Nos: What do you think prevented your progress? (Be as specific and honest as possible.)
Were there influences outside of your control? Were you resistant/how? Do you want to focus on this goal next month, or start a new one? All responses provide opportunities for growth.

Head to next month's intentions journal page (p.78) and write the goals and alchemy you will focus on for the next 30 days.

You will never change your life until you change something you do daily. The secret of your success is found in your daily routine.

- DARREN HARDY

{ finds joy in motivational speaking }

Month No. 1 *Your Free Space*

Create space for your dreams to materialize. As you journey, journal here about feelings, ideas, and next steps.

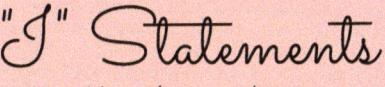

"I" Statements

Write positive and empowering messages.

Month No. 2

Envisioning Your Aim

*Imagination is everything. It is the preview
of life's coming attractions.*

- ALBERT EINSTEIN

{ found joy in physics }

Walking alongside the River of Dreams and following the tree marker way-finding signs, you are journeying further into the forest for your second month of exploration. Remember to go to a quiet place, and breathe deeply. Find a comfortable space within yourself where you feel centered, and can listen to your inner guide.

You are on the enchanted path and have reached lantern No. 2. You set down your travel bag that holds the keys to your joy and your intentions. You survey the area. At this rest stop, you spot a shining golden feather pen leaning up against the light post. With curiosity, you pick it up and look up at the bright blue sky. Imagining your destination, with the sky as your backdrop, you draw all you see in your mind's eye. You feel a sense of whimsy in your heart as you notice that the more beautiful details you sketch into your picture, the more it feels as if your dreams are materializing before you. This feeling of lightness allows you to keep expanding on your vision until the scene feels full.

In this second month of the journey, to support the transformation of your intentions into reality, I encourage you to envision your aims. Similar to professional athletes who practice visualizing a sequence of events in their mind's eye to train their mind-body-spirit for peak performance and winning, I invite you to visually assemble or write a script to support manifesting your heart's desires.

Svadhisthana is your second chakra, located at your sacral area. It is orange, representative of your emotional body, depth of feeling, sexuality, creativity, and the "I" statement, "I feel." This month you will connect to your creative center to manifest your dreams.

This exercise will help sharpen the focus of your binoculars to crystallize your dreams (*we are exploring*). It is used to cultivate your creative powers, and garner hope about your future. Moreover, your imaginative design will positively influence your thought patterns and belief systems. This is an important step forward because your mental patterns and belief systems create your reality.

Here are a few visualization techniques that I have found helpful. Select the one that speaks to you, or take these suggestions and create your own exercise. If you don't see your whole destination at the onset, start with the parts that you do perceive. The other elements will fill in as you set this project in motion and listen to your intuition. Remember your intuition is a built-in and *fail-safe compass* that is always steering you towards your highest and best path.

VISION BOARD

A vision board can help you create the life you want and give you the motivation and inspiration you need to achieve your goals.

- JACK CANFIELD

{ finds joy in motivation }

A vision board is a collection of images and words assembled together to symbolize the direction of your future. Think of the board like a Pinterest page. To assemble, gather a poster board along with magazines, newspapers, books that you are comfortable taking pages from (or make photocopies), photographs, and relevant printed images from the internet. Page through your sources and pull words, letters to create your words, and pictures that represent your intentions. Then, have fun cutting and pasting all you have collected onto the board.

Having a visual representation of your dreams will help you focus on and expand your attention. When you glance at your board you are emitting a positive frequency, working through limiting beliefs, and energetically attracting your desires. Observing joy with regularity is supportive in this pursuit. If you hear the voice of doubt creep into your mind, turn the thought around and remember, as Julia Cameron writes in *The Artist's Way*, "God has lots of money. God has lots of movie ideas, novel ideas, poems, songs, paintings, and acting jobs. God has a supply of loves, friends, houses that are all available to us." [7] Your work is to believe that what you have created on paper can and will materialize. Honor, too, that God/the Universe might have an even bigger plan for you that may exceed your expectations. Synchronicities abound when you are aligning with your true nature and believe you are a powerful co-creator.

One of my favorite vision board stories is relayed in the movie *The Secret*. A man realizes one day that the picture of the house he placed on his vision board years earlier is the exact home he is currently living in. I hope you have a similar experience and one day notice with absolute joy that the scene you pasted onto your board has come to fruition.

5 MAIN VISION BOARD ELEMENTS

1. Poster Board: consider where you will place your vision, and then purchase a board to fit that space.

2. Magazines: grab a handful of magazines that feel joyful.

3. Pictures: print pictures of your loved ones to add to your board if you wish.

4. Glue stick, glue dots, or double-sided tape: all options that will not crease your paper, or pictures, when adhering them to your board.

5. Scissors: you most likely will be cutting out letters to create words, so select scissors that feel comfortable in your hands.

MINI-MOVIE

Another idea is to create a mini-movie. Similar to a vision board, collect pictures, words, and inspirational quotes on your phone that depict your visions. Then, use an app like PicPlayPost or iMovie to create a video that captures your intentions. Replay your movie frequently, and add in music to elevate the feeling. The more you can emotionally connect to your dreams, the more supportive the exercise will be.

NOVELLA

Write about your dream life. Take time to think about how you want all the areas of your life to be and then describe your fabulous script in full detail as if you are a character in a novel. Get creative and channel the imagination portrayed in the movie *Ruby Sparks*!

LIFE TIMELINE

If you are more comfortable using a spreadsheet, write your script in the form of a timeline. On the left-hand side of the page, list the different areas of your life similar to the categories from Month No. 1 (Health, Home, Relationships, Career, Education, Finances, Community, Spirituality, and Leisure). On the top of the page, divide your life by decade extending to the right until you reach the legacy that you want to leave behind. Fill in the spreadsheet with your vision for each part of your life by the decade.

YOUR OBITUARY

This exercise is similar to writing your life novella, but it starts with your passing. Picture your life complete, and then fill in what is most important to have experienced while living, moving towards the present moment. Remember to keep the language positive.

My Visions Materialized

While writing this chapter, I found the box that houses my creative thoughts over the years. What I discovered in visioning work dating back over the past 15 years was enlightening. Many of my dreams have materialized, some in ways differently than I originally anticipated.

The meaningful morning routine I wrote about is now my foundational, and daily, spiritual reading, yoga, and meditation practice. I repeatedly wrote about eating more vegetables, and now I eat a primarily vegetarian diet. I wanted to drink less wine; I no longer drink wine. I hoped, again and again, that my health would improve. My 20+ year auto-immune disease pattern has healed. In 2006 I typed notes about a weekly family Sunday game night. I anticipated this game time being with my kids; my mom and I now play cribbage on-line on Sunday evenings. I created a children's clothing line in my thirties and aspired to have celebrity's children wear my line.

To support this dream, I pasted photos of my designs onto star style magazine pages featuring celebrity children. Angela Bassett and Courtney B. Vance's twins appeared on *The Oprah Winfrey Show* wearing hoodies from my line. One of my dream life scripts was written by decade and closed with legacy. Under legacy, I wrote these words: "Create a business that helps society," "Do what you love is possible." As well as, "Who is God?" I have created a business with a mission to help people thrive. I am doing what I love. One of the most significant shifts in my life has been gaining a better understanding of who God/the Universe is to me. As Mark Nepo describes so well in *Seven Thousand Ways to Listen*, "I let go of God as a directive force and discovered God by many names as the mysterious [loving] atmosphere in which we all live." [8] Seeing my dreams manifested as I look back through my previous vision work fills my heart with gratitude for the present, and hope for all of my current and future wishes.

Enjoy the process of creating your vision, and feel into your future with heartfelt passion. If you find these exercises cause you to think more deeply, modify your original intentions, and expand on your desires, be patient with yourself. This is an evolving process. The core of intentional living involves looking within and re-charting your path as you continue listening to your inner guidance. *Most importantly, when designing your life, stay faithful to your heart.*

Week No. 6 *Your Joy*

Cultivate joy! | Pay for the person behind you in line at the coffee shop!

Record moments of joy each day

What was your joy? Who/What gave rise to the joy? What did it feel, look, taste, smell, or sound like?

The process of reflective writing supports awareness. Awareness of what brings you joy serves as a heart-centered, resourceful compass, and unfolds more joy. The key to the journey is recognizing, understanding, and following -- your personal joy.

Joy Date · Write about your joy date - what you explored and how you felt.

Sunday _____

Monday _____

Tuesday _____

Wednesday _____

Thursday _____

Friday _____

Saturday _____

Week In Review

What was your most joyful moment this week? What themes, new or already noted, did you find in your joy moments?

The subjects have a wonderful story to tell you. And if you follow the essence -- more joy and purpose will come to light. Keep exploring your joy and add discoveries to your joy library.

Was any of your joy this week the product of working through fear and lessening your resistance towards a goal?

Recall scenarios where working through fear to reach a goal resulted in tremendous joy. With this awareness, in fearful moments you will find courage to move forward.

What were your achievements this week? Did you gain any new insights?

Note your most successful accomplishments, quality time with loved ones, and enlightening moments. Flip back periodically to honor your attentiveness to your priorities and review what you have learned.

Did you face challenges this week? Do you see different possibilities? How will you adjust moving forward?

Learning happens when you reflect and make adjustments to your course. Your growth is the product of working through struggles and finding a heart-centered solution. Joy resides here, too!

What kindness did you extend? How did you feel during and afterward?

Noting the kindness you extend during the week helps you to honor your light and love yourself more.

Use this space to begin planning for more joy in your life.

Dedicating time for joy makes your days brighter and more meaningful.

People

Places

Things

Experiences

Joy Date Ideas

Week No. 7 — *Your Joy*

Cultivate joy! | Say no to events that you "should" attend, and do something that fills you!

Record moments of joy each day | What was your joy? Who/What gave rise to the joy? What did it feel, look, taste, smell, or sound like?

The process of reflective writing supports awareness. Awareness of what brings you joy serves as a heart-centered, resourceful compass, and unfolds more joy. The key to the journey is recognizing, understanding, and following -- your personal joy.

Joy Date · Write about your joy date - what you explored and how you felt.

Sunday _____

Monday _____

Tuesday _____

Wednesday _____

Thursday _____

Friday _____

Saturday _____

Week In Review

What was your most joyful moment this week? What themes, new or already noted, did you find in your joy moments?

The subjects have a wonderful story to tell you. And if you follow the essence -- more joy and purpose will come to light. Keep exploring your joy and add discoveries to your joy library.

Was any of your joy this week the product of working through fear and lessening your resistance towards a goal?

Recall scenarios where working through fear to reach a goal resulted in tremendous joy. With this awareness, in fearful moments you will find courage to move forward.

What were your achievements this week? Did you gain any new insights?

Note your most successful accomplishments, quality time with loved ones, and enlightening moments. Flip back periodically to honor your attentiveness to your priorities and review what you have learned.

Did you face challenges this week? Do you see different possibilities? How will you adjust moving forward?

Learning happens when you reflect and make adjustments to your course. Your growth is the product of working through struggles and finding a heart-centered solution. Joy resides here, too!

What kindness did you extend? How did you feel during and afterward?

Noting the kindness you extend during the week helps you to honor your light and love yourself more.

Use this space to begin planning for more joy in your life.

Dedicating time for joy makes your days brighter and more meaningful.

People

Places

Things

Experiences

Joy Date Ideas

Week No. 8 *Your Joy*

Cultivate joy! | Let the person behind you at the store go before you!

Record moments of joy each day | What was your joy? Who/What gave rise to the joy? What did it feel, look, taste, smell, or sound like?

The process of reflective writing supports awareness. Awareness of what brings you joy serves as a heart-centered, resourceful compass, and unfolds more joy. The key to the journey is recognizing, understanding, and following -- your personal joy.

Joy Date · Write about your joy date - what you explored and how you felt.

_____

Sunday _____

_____

Monday _____

_____

Tuesday _____

_____

Wednesday _____

_____

Thursday _____

_____

Friday _____

_____

Saturday _____

_____

Week In Review

What was your most joyful moment this week? What themes, new or already noted, did you find in your joy moments?

The subjects have a wonderful story to tell you. And if you follow the essence -- more joy and purpose will come to light. Keep exploring your joy and add discoveries to your joy library.

Was any of your joy this week the product of working through fear and lessening your resistance towards a goal?

Recall scenarios where working through fear to reach a goal resulted in tremendous joy. With this awareness, in fearful moments you will find courage to move forward.

What were your achievements this week? Did you gain any new insights?

Note your most successful accomplishments, quality time with loved ones, and enlightening moments. Flip back periodically to honor your attentiveness to your priorities and review what you have learned.

Did you face challenges this week? Do you see different possibilities? How will you adjust moving forward?

Learning happens when you reflect and make adjustments to your course. Your growth is the product of working through struggles and finding a heart-centered solution. Joy resides here, too!

What kindness did you extend? How did you feel during and afterward?

Noting the kindness you extend during the week helps you to honor your light and love yourself more.

Use this space to begin planning for more joy in your life.

Dedicating time for joy makes your days brighter and more meaningful.

People

Places

Things

Experiences

Joy Date Ideas

Week No. 9 *Your Joy*

Cultivate joy! | Treat yourself to your favorite meal!

Record moments of joy each day

What was your joy? Who/What gave rise to the joy? What did it feel, look, taste, smell, or sound like?

The process of reflective writing supports awareness. Awareness of what brings you joy serves as a heart-centered, resourceful compass, and unfolds more joy. The key to the journey is recognizing, understanding, and following -- your personal joy.

Joy Date · Write about your joy date - what you explored and how you felt.

Sunday _____

Monday _____

Tuesday _____

Wednesday _____

Thursday _____

Friday _____

Saturday _____

Week In Review

What was your most joyful moment this week? What themes, new or already noted, did you find in your joy moments?

The subjects have a wonderful story to tell you. And if you follow the essence -- more joy and purpose will come to light. Keep exploring your joy and add discoveries to your joy library.

Was any of your joy this week the product of working through fear and lessening your resistance towards a goal?

Recall scenarios where working through fear to reach a goal resulted in tremendous joy. With this awareness, in fearful moments you will find courage to move forward.

What were your achievements this week? Did you gain any new insights?

Note your most successful accomplishments, quality time with loved ones, and enlightening moments. Flip back periodically to honor your attentiveness to your priorities and review what you have learned.

Did you face challenges this week? Do you see different possibilities? How will you adjust moving forward?

Learning happens when you reflect and make adjustments to your course. Your growth is the product of working through struggles and finding a heart-centered solution. Joy resides here, too!

What kindness did you extend? How did you feel during and afterward?

Noting the kindness you extend during the week helps you to honor your light and love yourself more.

Use this space to begin planning for more joy in your life.

Dedicating time for joy makes your days brighter and more meaningful.

People

Places

Things

Experiences

Joy Date Ideas

Your Intentions

YOUR KEYWORD

Along with your keyword, draw on the inner strength of curiosity, hope, and self-compassion as you approach your intentions.

Track the energy that you put towards your aspirations, and observe what is gained. Remember that being intentional about how you spend your time will help you achieve your goals. Where your attention goes, your energy flows.

No. 01

DESIRED GOAL:

ALCHEMY:

1	2	3	4	5	6	7
8	9	10	11	12	13	14
15	16	17	18	19	20	21
22	23	24	25	26	27	28
29	30	31				

No. 02

DESIRED GOAL:

ALCHEMY:

1	2	3	4	5	6	7
8	9	10	11	12	13	14
15	16	17	18	19	20	21
22	23	24	25	26	27	28
29	30	31				

No. 03

DESIRED GOAL:

ALCHEMY:

1	2	3	4	5	6	7
8	9	10	11	12	13	14
15	16	17	18	19	20	21
22	23	24	25	26	27	28
29	30	31				

No. 04

DESIRED GOAL:

ALCHEMY:

1	2	3	4	5	6	7
8	9	10	11	12	13	14
15	16	17	18	19	20	21
22	23	24	25	26	27	28
29	30	31				

Month In Review

Reflect on your time spent working towards your intentions.

Did you spend time as planned on your goals? Have you released what you needed to, and started to refine your focus? Record below a yes, partial, or no.

GOAL/ALCHEMY No. 01

GOAL/ALCHEMY No. 02

GOAL/ALCHEMY No. 03

GOAL/ALCHEMY No. 04

Those who attempt the absurd can achieve the impossible.

- ALBERT EINSTEIN
{ found joy in physics }

The yesses: Congratulations! Write about your successes.

How do you feel? What does this accomplishment offer you? If you no longer need to track this goal, consider introducing a new intention from your Month No. 1 exercise.

The partials: Is there anything new that you could implement that would help you achieve your goals?

Do you need to be more intentional in setting aside time for your desires? Do you need to break the goal down into smaller steps? Be kind to yourself as you process.

The Nos: What do you think prevented you? (Be as specific and honest as possible.)

Were there influences outside of your control? Were you resistant/how? Do you want to focus on this goal next month, or start a new one? All responses provide opportunities for growth.

Head to next month's intentions journal page (p.98) and write the goals and alchemy you will focus on for the next 30 days.

Month No. 2 *Your Free Space*

Create space for your dreams to materialize. As you journey, journal here about feelings, ideas, and next steps.

"I" Statements

Write positive and empowering messages.

Love

Eternity

Water Rest Area

Picnic Rest Area

Vista Rest Area

Month No. 3

Shining Light on Fear

I believe that every single event in life happens in an opportunity to choose love over fear.

- OPRAH WINFREY

{ finds joy in purpose }

On your path, you are walking closer inward towards the heart of the forest. Your journey so far has been blessed with beautiful weather, but as you approach the third glowing lantern, the skies darken, and gray storm clouds start rolling in. As you set down your travel bag, you say a prayer that the rain holds off. You begin to feel anxiety rising as you see no place to shelter if lightning and thunder start. Suddenly, you notice a magical magnifying glass perched up against this mile post's lantern. As you pick up the magnifying glass and examine its illuminated lens, you immediately think of several ways to keep safe on the trail during a storm. The sun begins to break through the clouds. You realize the magical magnifying glass is placed on your path to help you see your fear, and your strength, in a new light.

Fear is not real. It is a product of thoughts you create. Do not misunderstand me. Danger is real. But fear is a choice..

- WILL SMITH

{ finds joy in acting }

Yellow is the color of the third chakra. Located at your solar plexus, Manipura encompasses your self-esteem and your ego. Your ego and fear know each other well. This month you will deepen your ability to work through fear. "I act" is an "I" statement.

Often, when setting out on a new journey, the beginning feels exciting, and you are full of optimism. But, over time the adrenaline dissipates. You lose momentum and fear creeps in. Sometimes this avoidance (feeling of fear) is labeled 'lack of interest'. To keep moving towards your heart's desires, it is important to examine the origins of your fear.

The third month of the journey is dedicated to supporting your ability to work through fear. The Mayo Clinic defines fear as, "an unpleasant feeling triggered by the perception of danger, real or imagined." From the moment you wake up, to the time you lay your head to rest, you are perceiving, or sensing reality, and then making choices. Your choices, in the form of thoughts and actions, are rooted in love or fear. Sometimes at the fast pace that we exist in, we unconsciously pick the path that seems easiest or most comfortable. This is not always the path in love. Moving forward in love is elevating, but that decision can also feel uncomfortable. Here are several approaches that I find helpful to sort through my fears. These perspectives help me act from a place of awareness, and make more love-based decisions.

HAVE AN INSIGHTFUL CONVERSATION

Approaching fear with a compassionate and honest conversation can provide clarity. It helps to understand, first, if your fear is real or imagined. Then, lovingly listen to what your fear is telling you. When you examine your fears, you can see that fear is conveying a message that can guide you in the direction of love. The process equips you with insights that allow you to see a higher perspective and gain the strength you need to move towards your true aims. To examine your fear, drop into your heart space. Then, find the root cause of your fears. The conversation can go something like this:

1. What is the fear?

2. Is it a real or imagined danger?

3. If imagined danger, what is the truth statement? (Example below)

4. What are you afraid of, and what can you do to feel comfortable?

5. What is the source? There is benefit in looking at the source of the thought. In many instances you are carrying a limiting belief that does not belong to you, or you may be experiencing a trigger (which can feel like a Pavlovian response) from an old pattern or trauma that has yet to heal.

6. Finally, state the opportunity with gratitude.

I encourage you to look back at your intention notes from Month No. 1. What did you want to release? Those attributes are facets of your root fears. In order to arrive at your destination, you have to work through your fear. In Month No. 1, I referenced two personal intention statement examples. In the first example, I wanted to release self-doubt in order to feel confident. In the second, I wanted to release my fear of not having enough time to meditate in order to find clarity. Here are two outlines of conversations with these fears. As you read my examples and look at your fear, you might also find a common thread with growth opportunities. Everything is connected. This root fear will keep presenting itself in various forms until you heal it. God/the Universe wants you to shine. Sometimes like a parent, its voice gets louder in an attempt to help you. It is by bringing the magical magnifying glass over your fear that you can see the root illusion and do the healing work.

EXAMPLE NO. 1

1. What is the fear? *I experience self-doubt about writing a successful personal growth journal.*

2. Is this a real or imagined danger? *Imagined*

3. If imagined, what is the truth statement? *I can create a successful personal growth journal.*

4. What are you afraid of, and what can you do to feel comfortable? *I am afraid of failure. To feel comfortable I can listen to my heart and honor its guidance.*

5. What is the source? *The source is a pattern of self-doubt, and fear of expressing my true self.*

6. Finally, state the opportunity with gratitude. *This opportunity will provide me with clarity, confidence, and faith.*

1. What is the fear? *My fear is that I don't have enough time to meditate for 15 min each day.*

2. Is this a real or imagined danger? *Imagined*

3. If imagined, what is the truth statement? *I have time to meditate for 15 min each day.*

4. What are you afraid of, and what can you do to feel comfortable? *I am afraid of failure. To feel comfortable I can listen to my heart and honor its guidance.*

5. What is the source? *The source is a pattern of feeling like I am running out of time to succeed with all my aspirations.*

6. Finally, state the opportunity with gratitude. *This opportunity will provide me with clarity, confidence, and faith.*

Your Conversations with Fear

The following journal prompts provide space for you to write about your fears, turn them around constructively, and see the empowering and loving opportunity in them.

1. What is the fear?

2. Is it a real or imagined danger?

3. If imagined danger, what is the truth statement?

4. What are you afraid of, and what can you do to feel comfortable?

5. What is the source?

6. Finally, state the opportunity with gratitude.

1. What is the fear?

2. Is it a real or imagined danger?

3. If imagined danger, what is the truth statement?

4. What are you afraid of, and what can you do to feel comfortable?

5. What is the source?

6. Finally, state the opportunity with gratitude.

---

1. What is the fear?

2. Is it a real or imagined danger?

3. If imagined danger, what is the truth statement?

4. What are you afraid of, and what can you do to feel comfortable?

5. What is the source?

6. Finally, state the opportunity with gratitude.

---

1. What is the fear?

2. Is it a real or imagined danger?

3. If imagined danger, what is the truth statement?

4. What are you afraid of, and what can you do to feel comfortable?

5. What is the source?

6. Finally, state the opportunity with gratitude.

ENTER A JUDGMENT-FREE ZONE

Approach your fear with curiosity instead of judgment. Without judgment, there is less emotion. With less emotion, there is more rapid thought movement. You can also separate yourself from your fearful thoughts, picturing them floating by in a little cartoon bubble. This technique allows you to stay on your best course with more ease.

CREATE AN ENDEARING GREMLIN

If you have good thoughts they will shine out of your face like sunbeams and you will always look lovely.

- ROALD DAHL

{ found joy in writing }

You can also think of fear as a gremlin creature that is with you for the duration of your journey. Love this gremlin as if he is part of you. Remain aware of his location without letting him control the navigation. He might pop out from the trees and scare you periodically, or have a tantrum right in front of you on the path. Over time his expressions will become more endearing as you realize he is forever your companion.

MOVE, ALLOW SPACE TO SLOW DOWN, OR DO NOTHING

If you sense a heavy emotion related to a fearful thought and begin to feel overwhelmed, it can help to move, or practice grounding. In both instances, attention shifts away from your negative thought spiral and the fear-based feeling subsides. Or do nothing. I read something once that stated anxiety is telling you to either move or stop moving. I check in with that statement and find relief frequently. Giving yourself space to slow down, or rest, can bring you a great amount of comfort. Feel into which action your heart needs and honor it.

ATTUNE TO YOUR TRUE NATURE

The ego does not love you. It is unaware of who you are.

- A COURSE IN MIRACLES

Routinely set the intention to attune to your true nature; this might be the first thing in the morning before you open your eyes. Remember that your true nature is incapable of hurting you or anyone else. Our true nature is a state of love. It is the ego, or false self, that is creating the fear-based thinking. You can let your false self float away and choose to lean into love. By leaning away from pessimistic thinking and towards love - *and all the things that bring you joy -*

the rumination begins to lose its power. The fearful thoughts hurt less when you see them from this light. You are not your fearful thoughts. *You are love.*

CALL IN YOUR GUIDES

Your spiritual guides are waiting to help you. Simply stating what you need from them calls them to action. You most likely will feel a change in energy after this step, meaning something will shift so you feel better. In addition to a lighter experience, sometimes I feel a breeze or sense light. Become aware of what transpires after you ask your guides for help.

REMEMBER YOU ARE PART OF THE UNIVERSE

You are the universe, expressing itself as a human for a little while.

- ECKHART TOLLE

{ finds joy in personal evolution }

Acknowledging that your experience is happening through you, not to you, offers relief. Each being is an expression of God/the Universe, and God/the Universe has a lot to convey. Everyone faces doubt and frustration. We are here to grow, and working through fear is part of the process!

Remain true to yourself and your dreams. You are a shining star. Your most important work tends to be the hardest. To achieve your dreams, sometimes, you need to get comfortable being uncomfortable. Often, your edge is the place where you grow. Your job is to keep showing up with your heartfelt intentions. The more you dare to lovingly confront your fears, including your fear of other people's opinions, and release control, the more you will see fear dissolve. Doing the inner work to gain clarity will help you stay self-aware, centered, and aiming high. *There is always a healing solution awaiting you. Remember to place the magical magnifying glass over your fear to find the empowering light.*

Week No. 10 *Your Joy*

Cultivate joy! | Leave a bright note that says, "Wishing you a great day" on the windshield of several cars!

Record moments of joy each day | What was your joy? Who/What gave rise to the joy? What did it feel, look, taste, smell, or sound like?

The process of reflective writing supports awareness. Awareness of what brings you joy serves as a heart-centered, resourceful compass, and unfolds more joy. The key to the journey is recognizing, understanding, and following -- your personal joy.

Joy Date · Write about your joy date - what you explored and how you felt.

_____

Sunday _____

_____

Monday _____

_____

Tuesday _____

_____

Wednesday _____

_____

Thursday _____

_____

Friday _____

_____

Saturday _____

_____

Week In Review

What was your most joyful moment this week? What themes, new or already noted, did you find in your joy moments?

The subjects have a wonderful story to tell you. And if you follow the essence -- more joy and purpose will come to light. Keep exploring your joy and add discoveries to your joy library.

Was any of your joy this week the product of working through fear and lessening your resistance towards a goal?

Recall scenarios where working through fear to reach a goal resulted in tremendous joy. With this awareness, in fearful moments you will find courage to move forward.

What were your achievements this week? Did you gain any new insights?

Note your most successful accomplishments, quality time with loved ones, and enlightening moments. Flip back periodically to honor your attentiveness to your priorities and review what you have learned.

Did you face challenges this week? Do you see different possibilities? How will you adjust moving forward?

Learning happens when you reflect and make adjustments to your course. Your growth is the product of working through struggles and finding a heart-centered solution. Joy resides here, too!

What kindness did you extend? How did you feel during and afterward?

Noting the kindness you extend during the week helps you to honor your light and love yourself more.

Use this space to begin planning for more joy in your life.

Dedicating time for joy makes your days brighter and more meaningful.

People

Places

Things

Experiences

Joy Date Ideas

Week No. 11
Your Joy

Cultivate joy! | Spend extra time on your favorite hobby!

Record moments of joy each day

What was your joy? Who/What gave rise to the joy? What did it feel, look, taste, smell, or sound like?

The process of reflective writing supports awareness. Awareness of what brings you joy serves as a heart-centered, resourceful compass, and unfolds more joy. The key to the journey is recognizing, understanding, and following -- your personal joy.

Joy Date · Write about your joy date - what you explored and how you felt.

_____

Sunday _____

_____

Monday _____

_____

Tuesday _____

_____

Wednesday _____

_____

Thursday _____

_____

Friday _____

_____

Saturday _____

_____

Week In Review

What was your most joyful moment this week? What themes, new or already noted, did you find in your joy moments?

The subjects have a wonderful story to tell you. And if you follow the essence -- more joy and purpose will come to light. Keep exploring your joy and add discoveries to your joy library.

*If I love myself
I love you.
If I love you
I love myself.*

- RUMI
{ found joy in the mystical }

Was any of your joy this week the product of working through fear and lessening your resistance towards a goal?

Recall scenarios where working through fear to reach a goal resulted in tremendous joy. With this awareness, in fearful moments you will find courage to move forward.

What were your achievements this week? Did you gain any new insights?

Note your most successful accomplishments, quality time with loved ones, and enlightening moments. Flip back periodically to honor your attentiveness to your priorities and review what you have learned.

Did you face challenges this week? Do you see different possibilities? How will you adjust moving forward?

Learning happens when you reflect and make adjustments to your course. Your growth is the product of working through struggles and finding a heart-centered solution. Joy resides here, too!

What kindness did you extend? How did you feel during and afterward?

Noting the kindness you extend during the week helps you to honor your light and love yourself more.

Use this space to begin planning for more joy in your life.

Dedicating time for joy makes your days brighter and more meaningful.

People
Places
Things
Experiences
Joy Date Ideas

Week No. 12 *Your Joy*

Cultivate joy! | Write your partner, child, or friend a list of things you love about them!

Record moments of joy each day | What was your joy? Who/What gave rise to the joy? What did it feel, look, taste, smell, or sound like?

The process of reflective writing supports awareness. Awareness of what brings you joy serves as a heart-centered, resourceful compass, and unfolds more joy. The key to the journey is recognizing, understanding, and following -- your personal joy.

Joy Date · Write about your joy date - what you explored and how you felt.

Sunday _____

Monday _____

Tuesday _____

Wednesday _____

Thursday _____

Friday _____

Saturday _____

Week In Review

What was your most joyful moment this week? What themes, new or already noted, did you find in your joy moments?

The subjects have a wonderful story to tell you. And if you follow the essence -- more joy and purpose will come to light. Keep exploring your joy and add discoveries to your joy library.

Was any of your joy this week the product of working through fear and lessening your resistance towards a goal?

Recall scenarios where working through fear to reach a goal resulted in tremendous joy. With this awareness, in fearful moments you will find courage to move forward.

What were your achievements this week? Did you gain any new insights?

Note your most successful accomplishments, quality time with loved ones, and enlightening moments. Flip back periodically to honor your attentiveness to your priorities and review what you have learned.

Did you face challenges this week? Do you see different possibilities? How will you adjust moving forward?

Learning happens when you reflect and make adjustments to your course. Your growth is the product of working through struggles and finding a heart-centered solution. Joy resides here, too!

What kindness did you extend? How did you feel during and afterward?

Noting the kindness you extend during the week helps you to honor your light and love yourself more.

Use this space to begin planning for more joy in your life.

Dedicating time for joy makes your days brighter and more meaningful.

People

Places

Things

Experiences

Joy Date Ideas

Week No. 13 *Your Joy*

Cultivate joy! | Learn a new skill!

Record moments of joy each day

What was your joy? Who/What gave rise to the joy? What did it feel, look, taste, smell, or sound like?

The process of reflective writing supports awareness. Awareness of what brings you joy serves as a heart-centered, resourceful compass, and unfolds more joy. The key to the journey is recognizing, understanding, and following -- your personal joy.

Joy Date · Write about your joy date - what you explored and how you felt.

Sunday _____

Monday _____

Tuesday _____

Wednesday _____

Thursday _____

Friday _____

Saturday _____

Week In Review

What was your most joyful moment this week? What themes, new or already noted, did you find in your joy moments?

The subjects have a wonderful story to tell you. And if you follow the essence -- more joy and purpose will come to light. Keep exploring your joy and add discoveries to your joy library.

Was any of your joy this week the product of working through fear and lessening your resistance towards a goal?

Recall scenarios where working through fear to reach a goal resulted in tremendous joy. With this awareness, in fearful moments you will find courage to move forward.

What were your achievements this week? Did you gain any new insights?

Note your most successful accomplishments, quality time with loved ones, and enlightening moments. Flip back periodically to honor your attentiveness to your priorities and review what you have learned.

Did you face challenges this week? Do you see different possibilities? How will you adjust moving forward?

Learning happens when you reflect and make adjustments to your course. Your growth is the product of working through struggles and finding a heart-centered solution. Joy resides here, too!

What kindness did you extend? How did you feel during and afterward?

Noting the kindness you extend during the week helps you to honor your light and love yourself more.

Use this space to begin planning for more joy in your life.

Dedicating time for joy makes your days brighter and more meaningful.

People

Places

Things

Experiences

Joy Date Ideas

Your Intentions

YOUR KEYWORD

Along with your keyword, draw on the inner strength of curiosity, hope, and self-compassion as you approach your intentions.

Track the energy that you put towards your aspirations, and observe what is gained. Remember that being intentional about how you spend your time will help you achieve your goals. Where your attention goes, your energy flows.

No. 01
DESIRED GOAL:

ALCHEMY:

1	2	3	4	5	6	7
8	9	10	11	12	13	14
15	16	17	18	19	20	21
22	23	24	25	26	27	28
29	30	31				

No. 02
DESIRED GOAL:

ALCHEMY:

1	2	3	4	5	6	7
8	9	10	11	12	13	14
15	16	17	18	19	20	21
22	23	24	25	26	27	28
29	30	31				

No. 03
DESIRED GOAL:

ALCHEMY:

1	2	3	4	5	6	7
8	9	10	11	12	13	14
15	16	17	18	19	20	21
22	23	24	25	26	27	28
29	30	31				

No. 04
DESIRED GOAL:

ALCHEMY:

1	2	3	4	5	6	7
8	9	10	11	12	13	14
15	16	17	18	19	20	21
22	23	24	25	26	27	28
29	30	31				

Month In Review

Reflect on your time spent working towards your intentions.

Did you spend time as planned on your goals? Have you released what you needed to, and started to refine your focus? Record below a yes, partial, or no

GOAL/ALCHEMY No. 01

GOAL/ALCHEMY No. 02

GOAL/ALCHEMY No. 03

GOAL/ALCHEMY No. 04

Never give up on a dream just because of the time it will take to accomplish it. The time will pass anyway.

- EARL NIGHTINGALE

{ found joy in meaningful existence }

The yesses: Congratulations! Write about your successes.

How do you feel? What does this accomplishment offer you? If you no longer need to track this goal, consider introducing a new intention from your Month No. 1 exercise.

The partials: Is there anything new that you could implement that would help you achieve your goals?

Do you need to be more intentional in setting aside time for your desires? Do you need to break the goal down into smaller steps? Be kind to yourself as you process.

The Nos: What do you think prevented you? (Be as specific and honest as possible.)

Were there influences outside of your control? Were you resistant/how? Do you want to focus on this goal next month, or start a new one? All responses provide opportunities for growth.

Head to next month's intentions journal page (p.122) and write the goals and alchemy you will focus on for the next 30 days.

Month No. 3 *Your Free Space*

Create space for your dreams to materialize. As you journey, journal here about feelings, ideas, and next steps.

"I" Statements

Write positive and empowering messages.

Water Rest Area

At this part of the path, you arrive at a large diamond-shaped yellow sign that reads, "What's your water situation? Are you drinking enough water?!" A few strides further, you enter a rest area brimming with life. There is a breathtaking waterfall. The cascade's sound is captivating, and its reflection is opalescent. The falling water creates a brilliant pool. Across from the bright pool, you find a colorful canopy-covered kiosk resembling a lemonade stand at first glance and a resort bar at second glance. You walk closer and notice that here the forest offers you an assortment of fresh sliced fruits for your water and a carbonation station to add bubbles. Embellishing the resort atmosphere, in the air, you hear TLC singing "Waterfalls." You take the opportunity to dance like nobody's watching and then dive into the pool. After your dance party and refreshing swim, you refill your water bottles at the stand and reflect on the song's message. The seduction of shiny bling is a short-term detour. You continue again on your path, steadily walking towards your dreams along the rivers and lakes.

As you journey make sure you are drinking plenty of water. Your body consists of approximately 60% water. In addition to quenching your thirst, water aids bodily functions including digestion, circulation, creation of saliva, transportation of nutrients, and maintenance of ideal body temperature. Water energizes your muscles, supports healthy skin, and helps your kidneys process waste. [9] If you find that you avoid drinking water because it tastes dull to you, consider adding hydrating lemons, limes, or cucumbers. [10] Another option to try is reverse osmosis water free of larger particles. Or drink naturally carbonated mineral water that provides calcium, potassium, and magnesium.

WHERE JOY, INTENTION, AND WATER MEET

Among others, Masaru Emoto and Lynne McTaggart have studied the effects of how sending words, thoughts, and intention can impact the molecular structure of water. In *The New York Times* bestseller *The Hidden Messages in Water*, Masaru published his popular study on how water exposed to high vibrational thoughts, and then frozen, resulted in beautiful molecular formations. At the same time, water exposed to lower vibrational fear-based thoughts resulted in less attractive and more distorted crystal formations. [11] In a similar light, Lynne McTaggart has conducted extensive research and written several books on intention. In one study, she asked a group of people to send the thought "glow and glow" to a beaker of distilled water. Lynne and her scientific team connected this beaker and a control beaker to a device that was capable of measuring the spread of light, and the light's level of intensity, before, during, and after participants sent their intentions. The team "recorded a highly significant statistical difference in the spread of light and its intensity during the intention period and the period afterward, compared with measurements of the control beaker." The most significant impact was recorded during the 10 minute intention period. [12] Experiments like these help affirm that our thoughts are energy, and to whom and what we direct our thinking, including ourselves, really does matter.

My Experience with Intention Groups

Although not a documented or scientifically controlled experiment, I led a weekly intention group for 10 months that included nine members spanning the country and globe, eight people from New York to California, and one person from Nairobi. Each week we gathered and sent our concentrated healing thoughts for 10 minutes to a person in need. Many of the recipients experienced an outcome indicating our thoughts made a difference either during, and/or after the intention period.

Water is fluid, soft and yielding. But water will
wear away rock, which is rigid and cannot yield.
As a rule, whatever is fluid, soft and yielding
will overcome whatever is rigid and hard. This is
another paradox: what is soft is strong.

- LAU TZU

{ found joy in philosophy }

Month No. 4

Tidying, Decorating, and Blessing Your Home

Tidying is the act of confronting yourself. The process of discarding and organizing confronts your emotions about the past, as well as your fears about the future. Your stuff (things that bring you joy and things that don't) will show you what you value most in life.

- MARIE KONDO

{ finds joy in organizing }

You have reached the second quarter of the journey! You have collected new tools and yet, your travel bag remains light. You most likely feel lighter than you did at the onset of the adventure since you have gained clarity and unpacked some of your fears.

Do you ever return home from a vacation, see things around you differently, and have a newfound drive to rearrange your space? Imagine you are back on the winding path in the enchanted forest. As you approach lantern No. 4, you see a tiny replica of your home alongside the path. You are in a state of wonder, but it is true, somehow your living space, on a smaller scale, is here with you. At this moment, you are able to see your home from a new perspective, as an outsider. It's as if you are looking from above. You sit next to your dollhouse-sized home and with curiosity peer inside. What do you sense?

The fourth month is designed to create a sense of lightness within your home. Sometimes, you gather tangible things to find comfort for the short-term, and over time, those items weigh you down. The central principle of Feng Shui, a design governed by energy flow, is that we are connected to our environment. In Feng Shui, the home represents your life. The attic is your future possibilities, and the basement is your past and subconscious mind. The energy of your belongings influences your entirety. This month, I suggest releasing heaviness within your living space. The lighter energy in your home will open up space to feel more beauty and freedom. This sense of bright openness will aid your manifestations too. If

This month you will connect again to your Solar Plexus chakra. This energy center represents your mental state, your will, and the affirmation, "I can." Clearing space can bring up uncomfortable feelings, including resistance. You can tidy and make room for more of what you desire.

your home feels heavy or disorganized, focus on tidying. If your home is already free of clutter, consider redecorating to bring in a new, joyous energy.

You might also have aspirations of moving. Taking time to tidy and refresh your space will help with any plans to relocate. As I was tidying my home, I repurposed items, fixed what was broken, and completed several small decorating projects. After those tasks were complete, I felt prepared to move. My home received an offer before listing it, through word of mouth, and the sale closed in 30 days. I believe the sale process was plain sailing and swift because there was less attachment, less constriction, and less doubt. Momentum had been created for the future.

TIDY

If you want to fly, give up everything that weighs you down.

- TONI MORRISON

{ found joy in writing }

If you feel overwhelmed by your things, consider employing tidying. You can go about this by room or by category. Either route you choose, I recommend utilizing the feeling of joy as a tool to differentiate, as Marie Kondo suggests in *The Life-Changing Magic of Tidying Up*. You will discover that making decisions about what to keep and what to release is less challenging this way. Moreover, you will further practice attuning to your heart (as you are doing following your personal joy) and you will be able to more clearly process your connections. As you release items that no longer "spark joy," you open up space to move forward towards your desires with more ease. Some forms of energy you will shed include stagnation, overwhelm, feeling out of balance, and pain. That energy will transform into serenity, strength, freedom and flow. You will find that you can detach from the old you and better discern who you are *now*. Working your way through your living space and keeping only joyful and purposeful items creates spaciousness and a warmth both within your home and yourself. Even though you have less material, you feel more abundant. The process cultivates a welcoming and inspiring space for your true self.

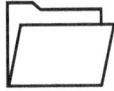 You may find that most of your items "spark joy". Excellent! You have a full life. My suggestion this month then is to focus on organizing your joy. As you organize your joy memories, consider creating folders for the years of your life and store your memorabilia chronologically.

DECORATE

If your home feels light, the suggestion this month is to introduce a refreshing project. The decorating project could be a new coat of paint in your office, a new rug for the dining room, an updated coffee table display, or rearrangement of your furniture. The project doesn't need to be on a grand scale. The concept is to make a pleasing, revitalizing, energetic shift in your home that will create a new perspective, and be a beautiful change. Where in your home do you feel the most uncomfortable? What room feels uninspiring? Where do you spend the least amount of time? Think about areas you avoid, and perhaps work on that space. Remember that all parts of your home represent all parts of you. A trip to the bookstore, magazine stand, or time on Pinterest to search for inspiring decorating ideas can be an uplifting joy date.

ASSISTANCE

These suggestions might feel like too much to do alone. If so, consider enlisting or hiring someone to help you. Most likely, the process will move much faster than you anticipate. You might even feel more ease and joy with a friend or an expert by your side.

In addition to physically tidying or decorating your home, try "smudging" with two natural elements that help clear stuck energy and bring in the energy of blessings: sage and the wood Palo Santo. I propose you use both after your projects to raise the vibration of your space. Sage and Palo Santo also make for a meaningful practice to routinely incorporate into your life.

SAGE

A sage stick is a bundle of the herb sage. The herb is dried and bound together with twine. Burning sage, also known as smudging, is a Native American spiritual ritual. It is used as a technique to cleanse a space of stagnant energy. It is believed that when sage is burned, it releases negative ions that clear the air of allergens. Negative ions are also thought to be mood boosters. I encourage intention setting when burning. Set the intention that the energy of sage will help clear the air and cleanse your space. Light one end of the stick, allow it to burn, then blow it out so the stick smokes. When addressing the energy of your house, start at your front door, and walk through each room of the house, holding the intention to release negative energy. You may want to open your doors and windows to further release the smoke and old energy. Saging can feel grounding. Sage spray and sage incense sticks are an alternative option to smudging. I often burn sage after energy sessions to clear the air of old energy released from the work.

PALO SANTO

Palo Santo is a sacred wood native to South America. Its name translates to holy wood. Palo Santo has healing and air clearing properties. The scent of Palo Santo is calming and relaxing. When using Palo Santo, similar to using sage, I suggest setting intentions. Set the intention for blessings, then, light your Palo Santo stick and allow it to catch fire. If a flame remains, blow the fire out so that the wood begins to smoke. Start at your front door and walk through each room of the house, thinking about peace, love, gratitude, and joy. Blessing your space in this manner creates a graceful vibration. Palo Santo can also be found in spray and incense stick form. I bless each Flourish product with the energy of Palo Santo before it is delivered.

In a harmonious living space you are more organized, peaceful, and intuitive. You develop a better appreciation for what you own, and become more thoughtful about your purchases. In a light home, you feel supported, more present, and have extra time for doing the things that bring you joy.

Have nothing in your home that you don't know to be useful or believe to be beautiful.

- WILLIAM MORRIS

{ found joy in textile design }

Week No. 14 *Your Joy*

Cultivate joy! | Share your gratitude with someone who has made a difference in your life!

Record moments of joy each day | What was your joy? Who/What gave rise to the joy? What did it feel, look, taste, smell, or sound like?

The process of reflective writing supports awareness. Awareness of what brings you joy serves as a heart-centered, resourceful compass, and unfolds more joy. The key to the journey is recognizing, understanding, and following -- your personal joy.

Joy Date · Write about your joy date - what you explored and how you felt.

_____

Sunday _____

_____

Monday _____

_____

Tuesday _____

_____

Wednesday _____

_____

Thursday _____

_____

Friday _____

_____

Saturday _____

_____

Week In Review

What was your most joyful moment this week? What themes, new or already noted, did you find in your joy moments?

The subjects have a wonderful story to tell you. And if you follow the essence -- more joy and purpose will come to light. Keep exploring your joy and add discoveries to your joy library.

A joyful heart is the normal result of a heart burning with love. She gives most who gives with joy.

- MOTHER TERESA

{ found joy in service }

Was any of your joy this week the product of working through fear and lessening your resistance towards a goal?

Recall scenarios where working through fear to reach a goal resulted in tremendous joy. With this awareness, in fearful moments you will find courage to move forward.

What were your achievements this week? Did you gain any new insights?

Note your most successful accomplishments, quality time with loved ones, and enlightening moments. Flip back periodically to honor your attentiveness to your priorities and review what you have learned.

Did you face challenges this week? Do you see different possibilities? How will you adjust moving forward?

Learning happens when you reflect and make adjustments to your course. Your growth is the product of working through struggles and finding a heart-centered solution. Joy resides here, too!

What kindness did you extend? How did you feel during and afterward?

Noting the kindness you extend during the week helps you to honor your light and love yourself more.

Use this space to begin planning for more joy in your life.

Dedicating time for joy makes your days brighter and more meaningful.

People

Places

Things

Experiences

Joy Date Ideas

Week No. 15 *Your Joy*

Cultivate joy! | Buy yourself a bouquet of flowers and a decadent chocolate bar, or other treat!

Record moments of joy each day | What was your joy? Who/What gave rise to the joy? What did it feel, look, taste, smell, or sound like?

The process of reflective writing supports awareness. Awareness of what brings you joy serves as a heart-centered, resourceful compass, and unfolds more joy. The key to the journey is recognizing, understanding, and following -- your personal joy.

Joy Date · Write about your joy date - what you explored and how you felt.

_____

_____

Sunday _____

_____

_____

Monday _____

_____

_____

Tuesday _____

_____

_____

Wednesday _____

_____

_____

Thursday _____

_____

_____

Friday _____

_____

_____

Saturday _____

_____

_____

Week In Review

What was your most joyful moment this week? What themes, new or already noted, did you find in your joy moments?

The subjects have a wonderful story to tell you. And if you follow the essence -- more joy and purpose will come to light. Keep exploring your joy and add discoveries to your joy library.

Was any of your joy this week the product of working through fear and lessening your resistance towards a goal?

Recall scenarios where working through fear to reach a goal resulted in tremendous joy. With this awareness, in fearful moments you will find courage to move forward.

What were your achievements this week? Did you gain any new insights?

Note your most successful accomplishments, quality time with loved ones, and enlightening moments. Flip back periodically to honor your attentiveness to your priorities and review what you have learned.

Did you face challenges this week? Do you see different possibilities? How will you adjust moving forward?

Learning happens when you reflect and make adjustments to your course. Your growth is the product of working through struggles and finding a heart-centered solution. Joy resides here, too!

What kindness did you extend? How did you feel during and afterward?

Noting the kindness you extend during the week helps you to honor your light and love yourself more.

Use this space to begin planning for more joy in your life.

Dedicating time for joy makes your days brighter and more meaningful.

People

Places

Things

Experiences

Joy Date Ideas

Week No. 16   *Your Joy*

Cultivate joy! | Purchase a box of nutrition bars to keep in your car, and give to the homeless!

Record moments of joy each day | What was your joy? Who/What gave rise to the joy? What did it feel, look, taste, smell, or sound like?

The process of reflective writing supports awareness. Awareness of what brings you joy serves as a heart-centered, resourceful compass, and unfolds more joy. The key to the journey is recognizing, understanding, and following -- your personal joy.

Joy Date · Write about your joy date - what you explored and how you felt.

_____

Sunday _____

_____

Monday _____

_____

Tuesday _____

_____

Wednesday _____

_____

Thursday _____

_____

Friday _____

_____

Saturday _____

_____

Week In Review

What was your most joyful moment this week? What themes, new or already noted, did you find in your joy moments?

The subjects have a wonderful story to tell you. And if you follow the essence -- more joy and purpose will come to light. Keep exploring your joy and add discoveries to your joy library.

There are souls in this world who have the gift of finding joy everywhere, and leaving it behind them when they go.

- FREDRICK WILLIAM FABER

{ found joy in hymns }

Was any of your joy this week the product of working through fear and lessening your resistance towards a goal?

Recall scenarios where working through fear to reach a goal resulted in tremendous joy. With this awareness, in fearful moments you will find courage to move forward.

What were your achievements this week? Did you gain any new insights?

Note your most successful accomplishments, quality time with loved ones, and enlightening moments. Flip back periodically to honor your attentiveness to your priorities and review what you have learned.

Did you face challenges this week? Do you see different possibilities? How will you adjust moving forward?

Learning happens when you reflect and make adjustments to your course. Your growth is the product of working through struggles and finding a heart-centered solution. Joy resides here, too!

What kindness did you extend? How did you feel during and afterward?

Noting the kindness you extend during the week helps you to honor your light and love yourself more.

Use this space to begin planning for more joy in your life.

Dedicating time for joy makes your days brighter and more meaningful.

People

Places

Things

Experiences

Joy Date Ideas

Week No. 17 *Your Joy*

Cultivate joy! | Take the backroads!

Record moments of joy each day

What was your joy? Who/What gave rise to the joy? What did it feel, look, taste, smell, or sound like?

The process of reflective writing supports awareness. Awareness of what brings you joy serves as a heart-centered, resourceful compass, and unfolds more joy. The key to the journey is recognizing, understanding, and following -- your personal joy.

Joy Date · Write about your joy date - what you explored and how you felt.

Sunday _____

Monday _____

Tuesday _____

Wednesday _____

Thursday _____

Friday _____

Saturday _____

Week In Review

What was your most joyful moment this week? What themes, new or already noted, did you find in your joy moments?

The subjects have a wonderful story to tell you. And if you follow the essence -- more joy and purpose will come to light. Keep exploring your joy and add discoveries to your joy library.

Was any of your joy this week the product of working through fear and lessening your resistance towards a goal?

Recall scenarios where working through fear to reach a goal resulted in tremendous joy. With this awareness, in fearful moments you will find courage to move forward.

What were your achievements this week? Did you gain any new insights?

Note your most successful accomplishments, quality time with loved ones, and enlightening moments. Flip back periodically to honor your attentiveness to your priorities and review what you have learned.

Did you face challenges this week? Do you see different possibilities? How will you adjust moving forward?

Learning happens when you reflect and make adjustments to your course. Your growth is the product of working through struggles and finding a heart-centered solution. Joy resides here, too!

What kindness did you extend? How did you feel during and afterward?

Noting the kindness you extend during the week helps you to honor your light and love yourself more.

Use this space to begin planning for more joy in your life.

Dedicating time for joy makes your days brighter and more meaningful.

People

Places

Things

Experiences

Joy Date Ideas

Week No. 18  Your Joy

Cultivate joy! | Spend time at a local bookshop!

Record moments of joy each day | What was your joy? Who/What gave rise to the joy? What did it feel, look, taste, smell, or sound like?

The process of reflective writing supports awareness. Awareness of what brings you joy serves as a heart-centered, resourceful compass, and unfolds more joy. The key to the journey is recognizing, understanding, and following -- your personal joy.

Joy Date · Write about your joy date - what you explored and how you felt.

_____

Sunday _____

Monday _____

Tuesday _____

Wednesday _____

Thursday _____

Friday _____

Saturday _____

Week In Review

What was your most joyful moment this week? What themes, new or already noted, did you find in your joy moments?

The subjects have a wonderful story to tell you. And if you follow the essence -- more joy and purpose will come to light. Keep exploring your joy and add discoveries to your joy library.

Was any of your joy this week the product of working through fear and lessening your resistance towards a goal?

Recall scenarios where working through fear to reach a goal resulted in tremendous joy. With this awareness, in fearful moments you will find courage to move forward.

What were your achievements this week? Did you gain any new insights?

Note your most successful accomplishments, quality time with loved ones, and enlightening moments. Flip back periodically to honor your attentiveness to your priorities and review what you have learned.

Did you face challenges this week? Do you see different possibilities? How will you adjust moving forward?

Learning happens when you reflect and make adjustments to your course. Your growth is the product of working through struggles and finding a heart-centered solution. Joy resides here, too!

What kindness did you extend? How did you feel during and afterward?

Noting the kindness you extend during the week helps you to honor your light and love yourself more.

Use this space to begin planning for more joy in your life.

Dedicating time for joy makes your days brighter and more meaningful.

People

Places

Things

Experiences

Joy Date Ideas

Month No. 4 *Your Intentions*

YOUR KEYWORD

Along with your keyword, draw on the inner strength of curiosity, hope, and self-compassion as you approach your intentions.

Track the energy that you put towards your aspirations, and observe what is gained. Remember that being intentional about how you spend your time will help you achieve your goals. Where your attention goes, your energy flows.

No. 01
DESIRED GOAL:

ALCHEMY:

1	2	3	4	5	6	7
8	9	10	11	12	13	14
15	16	17	18	19	20	21
22	23	24	25	26	27	28
29	30	31				

No. 02
DESIRED GOAL:

ALCHEMY:

1	2	3	4	5	6	7
8	9	10	11	12	13	14
15	16	17	18	19	20	21
22	23	24	25	26	27	28
29	30	31				

No. 03
DESIRED GOAL:

ALCHEMY:

1	2	3	4	5	6	7
8	9	10	11	12	13	14
15	16	17	18	19	20	21
22	23	24	25	26	27	28
29	30	31				

No. 04
DESIRED GOAL:

ALCHEMY:

1	2	3	4	5	6	7
8	9	10	11	12	13	14
15	16	17	18	19	20	21
22	23	24	25	26	27	28
29	30	31				

Month In Review

Reflect on your time spent working towards your intentions.

Did you spend time as planned on your goals? Have you released what you needed to, and started to refine your focus? Record below a yes, partial, or no.

GOAL/ALCHEMY No. 01

GOAL/ALCHEMY No. 02

GOAL/ALCHEMY No. 03

GOAL/ALCHEMY No. 04

The yesses: Congratulations! Write about your successes.

How do you feel? What does this accomplishment offer you? If you no longer need to track this goal, consider introducing a new intention from your Month No. 1 exercise.

The partials: Is there anything new that you could implement that would help you achieve your goals?

Do you need to be more intentional in setting aside time for your desires? Do you need to break the goal down into smaller steps? Be kind to yourself as you process.

The Nos: What do you think prevented you? (Be as specific and honest as possible.)

Were there influences outside of your control? Were you resistant/how? Do you want to focus on this goal next month, or start a new one? All responses provide opportunities for growth.

Head to next month's intentions journal page (p.140) and write the goals and alchemy you will focus on for the next 30 days.

Month No. 4 *Your Free Space*

Create space for your dreams to materialize. As you journey, journal here about feelings, ideas, and next steps.

"I" Statements

Write positive and empowering messages.

Love

Eternity

💧 Water Rest Area

⛱ Picnic Rest Area

Vista Rest Area

Month No. 5

Caring for Yourself

*You are always with yourself, so you might
as well enjoy the company.*

- DIANE VON FURSTENBERG

{ finds joy in design }

Today is a gorgeous day on the trail. You feel a joyful silence within as you approach mile-marker No. 5. You are almost to the half-way point of the journey. Hopefully, you have gained many of your desires and shed some - or all - of what no longer serves you.

You are feeling more clear, empowered, and excited to experience the gift of this delightful rest stop. The light of lantern No. 5 is incandescent. The brilliance of this lantern is more like a lighthouse. As you approach, you see a mirror wrapped in flowers resting up against a tree. This mirror has special powers. You quickly discover that when you place the mirror in front of your heart, you and only you can see what your heart is saying. Even more exciting is that when you listen to its direction, life feels magical. You think where has this mirror been all my life? Within you, the forest responds. You are a bit startled at the response but smile and realize that you and the forest seem to be more connected now too. Take some time and enjoy your discovery. In your mind's eye, practice holding the mirror in front of your heart, ask it questions and see what it reflects for you. Now imagine following its direction and feel into that experience.

The fifth chapter is formatted to help you better communicate with your heart. Self-care is not always easy, as it involves taking time to nurture yourself. Sometimes we place ourselves lower on our priority list. The foundation of self-care is the innate knowledge of how best to honor your personal needs. You will have noticed that the weekly acts of kindness suggestions rotate between forms of kindness towards others and towards yourself. Hopefully, you have allowed yourself to enjoy some small luxuries that you might not have otherwise. In this fifth month, the intention is to incorporate a robust self-care practice into your daily routine. What did your heart say to you when you picked up the mirror and asked questions? Those messages are guidance for you to follow this month too.

This month, instead of highlighting a chakra, the page color correlates to a gemstone. Pink is representative of Rose Quartz, the stone of unconditional love. Self-care is integral to loving yourself - unconditionally - and living a life full of joy. A supportive "I" statement this month is "I am worthy."

What I Have Learned About Self-Care

Self-care goes beyond a manicure and pedicure which is how I initially categorized the concept up until the past few years. The term self-care was coined in the middle of the 20th century to describe activities, such as exercise and grooming, that offered institutionalized patients an opportunity to maintain independence and nourish their self-worth. A decade later, first-responders started incorporating self-care practices into their daily lives to help manage PTSD symptoms. Care activities expanded to encompass a healthy diet, restful sleep, journaling, meditation, spirituality, and time spent in nature. In the 1970s, the Black Panther Party further popularized the term, advocating self-care for all Black citizens to remain healthy when faced with medical racism. [13]

The difference between successful people and really successful people is that really successful people say 'no' to almost everything.

- WARREN BUFFET

{ finds joy in investing }

Self-care is about investing in yourself and being able to make, and believe in, your own choices. A common theme in my life has been compromising my desires to accommodate other people due to fear of conflict and the uncomfortable feelings that arise, concern surrounding hurting someone else, being afraid of rejection, and lack of faith in myself. This pattern has not served me and has therefore become one of my biggest lessons. Saying no or expressing my differing opinion has been, frankly, scary. It has taken me years to learn that when I say yes falsely, as a way to avoid hurting someone else - that I injure myself instead. At the root, a fear of saying no is due to believing that love is conditional - which is false. This fear is rooted in a belief system of limited abundance - another falsehood. I have learned by working through my fears and observing the outcome of saying no, that my self-loving response steers me away from undue anxiety and towards inner peace.

CULTIVATE HEALTHY BOUNDARIES

This month, practice yielding to your heart's advice when it says no, or if you hear yourself say the red flag of "I should". Your heart is speaking to help you - to steer you towards love. If saying no frightens you, consider saying no as an experiment, or pull out your magical magnifying glass and examine why you are fearful of saying no. Remember, you can always make a different choice in the future. The clearer you are about why you are saying no, the more empowered you become. Over time it becomes easier as you experience the benefits of following your intuition. Instead of worrying about the outcome you fear, I encourage you to focus on what you desire. Then, become aware of what transpires. You most likely will be pleasantly surprised that unconditional love and abundance manifest as well as supportive synchronicities. As you cultivate self-awareness, you become more empowered to continue stating your truth.

It's not selfish to love yourself, take care of yourself and to make your happiness a priority. It's necessary.

- MANDY HALE
{ finds joy in empowering others }

PRACTICE PAMPERING YOURSELF UNTIL YOU FEEL FULL

The second suggested exercise for this month is to survey your current self-care activities and make loving adjustments. Create a plan so, at the end of the week, you can honestly say you took care of you. Keep in mind that self-care does not need to require spending a lot of money. You can find small pleasures and joy to fill you. Amidst the busyness of your day, listen to your heart and make choices that feel good, such as taking an extra 15 minutes to eat your lunch outside in the sunshine, or soaking in an Epsom salt bath before you go to sleep. As time goes on, a more loving, present, and whole version of yourself will come into fruition. If you find yourself hesitating to participate in self-care, or if you feel guilty while doing so, pull out the magical magnifying glass and find the root of your fear. I propose that you permit yourself to keep focusing on your self-care plan until you feel 100% satisfied with your routine.

Your Self-Care Practices

Included is a list of self-care suggestions to reflect on, and a weekly self-care calendar to support your creation of a personal best self-care plan. The calendar design is inspired by Day Designer's "My Favorite Self-Care Habits" printable.

Take time for what is joyful	Watch a movie
Spend time in nature	Read what you enjoy
Take a relaxing bath	Take yourself on a date
Go to bed early	Remove the shoulds on your list
Sleep in late	Say no to what you do not want
Nap	Take breaks during the workday
Meditate	Connect with loved ones
Cook nurturing food	Make time for your hobby
Get a massage	Exercise
Get a manicure-pedicure	Follow your heart spontaneously

You have been criticizing yourself for years and it hasn't worked. Try approving of yourself and see what happens.

- LOUISE L. HAY

{ found joy in self-empowerment }

Caring for yourself supports all parts of you: physical, emotional, mental, and spiritual. If you struggle with self-love and self-worth, taking time routinely for self-care might be challenging, but it is the best form of love you can show yourself. *Your most important relationship is the one you have with yourself.*

Your Personal Best Self-Care Plan

M	T	W	T	F	S	S	SELF-CARE PRACTICES

Week No. 19

Your Joy

Cultivate joy! | Leave a note of gratitude for your mail carrier!

Record moments of joy each day | What was your joy? Who/What gave rise to the joy? What did it feel, look, taste, smell, or sound like?

The process of reflective writing supports awareness. Awareness of what brings you joy serves as a heart-centered, resourceful compass, and unfolds more joy. The key to the journey is recognizing, understanding, and following -- your personal joy.

Joy Date · Write about your joy date - what you explored and how you felt.

Sunday _____

Monday _____

Tuesday _____

Wednesday _____

Thursday _____

Friday _____

Saturday _____

Week In Review

What was your most joyful moment this week? What themes, new or already noted, did you find in your joy moments?

The subjects have a wonderful story to tell you. And if you follow the essence -- more joy and purpose will come to light. Keep exploring your joy and add discoveries to your joy library.

Was any of your joy this week the product of working through fear and lessening your resistance towards a goal?

Recall scenarios where working through fear to reach a goal resulted in tremendous joy. With this awareness, in fearful moments you will find courage to move forward.

What were your achievements this week? Did you gain any new insights?

Note your most successful accomplishments, quality time with loved ones, and enlightening moments. Flip back periodically to honor your attentiveness to your priorities and review what you have learned.

Did you face challenges this week? Do you see different possibilities? How will you adjust moving forward?

Learning happens when you reflect and make adjustments to your course. Your growth is the product of working through struggles and finding a heart-centered solution. Joy resides here, too!

What kindness did you extend? How did you feel during and afterward?

Noting the kindness you extend during the week helps you to honor your light and love yourself more.

Use this space to begin planning for more joy in your life.

Dedicating time for joy makes your days brighter and more meaningful.

People

Places

Things

Experiences

Joy Date Ideas

Week No. 20 — *Your Joy*

Cultivate joy! | Do that thing you have always wanted to do!

Record moments of joy each day | What was your joy? Who/What gave rise to the joy? What did it feel, look, taste, smell, or sound like?

The process of reflective writing supports awareness. Awareness of what brings you joy serves as a heart-centered, resourceful compass, and unfolds more joy. The key to the journey is recognizing, understanding, and following -- your personal joy.

Joy Date · Write about your joy date - what you explored and how you felt.

Sunday _____

Monday _____

Tuesday _____

Wednesday _____

Thursday _____

Friday _____

Saturday _____

Week In Review

What was your most joyful moment this week? What themes, new or already noted, did you find in your joy moments?

The subjects have a wonderful story to tell you. And if you follow the essence -- more joy and purpose will come to light. Keep exploring your joy and add discoveries to your joy library.

The things that excite you are not random. They are connected to your purpose. Follow them.

- TERRIE DAVOLL HUDSON
{ finds joy in advocating }

Was any of your joy this week the product of working through fear and lessening your resistance towards a goal?

Recall scenarios where working through fear to reach a goal resulted in tremendous joy. With this awareness, in fearful moments you will find courage to move forward.

What were your achievements this week? Did you gain any new insights?

Note your most successful accomplishments, quality time with loved ones, and enlightening moments. Flip back periodically to honor your attentiveness to your priorities and review what you have learned.

Did you face challenges this week? Do you see different possibilities? How will you adjust moving forward?

Learning happens when you reflect and make adjustments to your course. Your growth is the product of working through struggles and finding a heart-centered solution. Joy resides here, too!

What kindness did you extend? How did you feel during and afterward?

Noting the kindness you extend during the week helps you to honor your light and love yourself more.

Use this space to begin planning for more joy in your life.

Dedicating time for joy makes your days brighter and more meaningful.

People
Places
Things
Experiences
Joy Date Ideas

Week No. 21 Your Joy

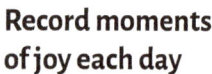

Cultivate joy! | When you open your inbox, write someone an encouraging email!

Record moments of joy each day | What was your joy? Who/What gave rise to the joy? What did it feel, look, taste, smell, or sound like?

The process of reflective writing supports awareness. Awareness of what brings you joy serves as a heart-centered, resourceful compass, and unfolds more joy. The key to the journey is recognizing, understanding, and following -- your personal joy.

Joy Date · Write about your joy date - what you explored and how you felt.

Sunday _____

Monday _____

Tuesday _____

Wednesday _____

Thursday _____

Friday _____

Saturday _____

Week In Review

What was your most joyful moment this week? What themes, new or already noted, did you find in your joy moments?

The subjects have a wonderful story to tell you. And if you follow the essence -- more joy and purpose will come to light. Keep exploring your joy and add discoveries to your joy library.

Was any of your joy this week the product of working through fear and lessening your resistance towards a goal?

Recall scenarios where working through fear to reach a goal resulted in tremendous joy. With this awareness, in fearful moments you will find courage to move forward.

What were your achievements this week? Did you gain any new insights?

Note your most successful accomplishments, quality time with loved ones, and enlightening moments. Flip back periodically to honor your attentiveness to your priorities and review what you have learned.

Did you face challenges this week? Do you see different possibilities? How will you adjust moving forward?

Learning happens when you reflect and make adjustments to your course. Your growth is the product of working through struggles and finding a heart-centered solution. Joy resides here, too!

What kindness did you extend? How did you feel during and afterward?

Noting the kindness you extend during the week helps you to honor your light and love yourself more.

Use this space to begin planning for more joy in your life.

Dedicating time for joy makes your days brighter and more meaningful.

People

Places

Things

Experiences

Joy Date Ideas

Week No. 22 *Your Joy*

Cultivate joy! | Buy yourself a new set of pens and/or markers!

Record moments of joy each day | What was your joy? Who/What gave rise to the joy? What did it feel, look, taste, smell, or sound like?

The process of reflective writing supports awareness. Awareness of what brings you joy serves as a heart-centered, resourceful compass, and unfolds more joy. The key to the journey is recognizing, understanding, and following -- your personal joy.

Joy Date · Write about your joy date - what you explored and how you felt.

Sunday _____

Monday _____

Tuesday _____

Wednesday _____

Thursday _____

Friday _____

Saturday _____

Week In Review

What was your most joyful moment this week? What themes, new or already noted, did you find in your joy moments?

The subjects have a wonderful story to tell you. And if you follow the essence -- more joy and purpose will come to light. Keep exploring your joy and add discoveries to your joy library.

Was any of your joy this week the product of working through fear and lessening your resistance towards a goal?

Recall scenarios where working through fear to reach a goal resulted in tremendous joy. With this awareness, in fearful moments you will find courage to move forward.

What were your achievements this week? Did you gain any new insights?

Note your most successful accomplishments, quality time with loved ones, and enlightening moments. Flip back periodically to honor your attentiveness to your priorities and review what you have learned.

Did you face challenges this week? Do you see different possibilities? How will you adjust moving forward?

Learning happens when you reflect and make adjustments to your course. Your growth is the product of working through struggles and finding a heart-centered solution. Joy resides here, too!

What kindness did you extend? How did you feel during and afterward?

Noting the kindness you extend during the week helps you to honor your light and love yourself more.

Use this space to begin planning for more joy in your life.

Dedicating time for joy makes your days brighter and more meaningful.

People

Places

Things

Experiences

Joy Date Ideas

YOUR KEYWORD

Along with your keyword, draw on the inner strength of curiosity, hope, and self-compassion as you approach your intentions.

Track the energy that you put towards your aspirations, and observe what is gained. Remember that being intentional about how you spend your time will help you achieve your goals. Where your attention goes, your energy flows.

No. 01

DESIRED GOAL:

ALCHEMY:

1	2	3	4	5	6	7
8	9	10	11	12	13	14
15	16	17	18	19	20	21
22	23	24	25	26	27	28
29	30	31				

No. 02

DESIRED GOAL:

ALCHEMY:

1	2	3	4	5	6	7
8	9	10	11	12	13	14
15	16	17	18	19	20	21
22	23	24	25	26	27	28
29	30	31				

No. 03

DESIRED GOAL:

ALCHEMY:

1	2	3	4	5	6	7
8	9	10	11	12	13	14
15	16	17	18	19	20	21
22	23	24	25	26	27	28
29	30	31				

No. 04

DESIRED GOAL:

ALCHEMY:

1	2	3	4	5	6	7
8	9	10	11	12	13	14
15	16	17	18	19	20	21
22	23	24	25	26	27	28
29	30	31				

Month In Review

Reflect on your time spent working towards your intentions.

Did you spend time as planned on your goals? Have you released what you needed to, and started to refine your focus? Record below a yes, partial, or no.

GOAL/ALCHEMY No. 01

GOAL/ALCHEMY No. 02

GOAL/ALCHEMY No. 03

GOAL/ALCHEMY No. 04

The yesses: Congratulations! Write about your successes.

How do you feel? What does this accomplishment offer you? If you no longer need to track this goal, consider introducing a new intention from your Month No. 1 exercise.

The partials: Is there anything new that you could implement that would help you achieve your goals?

Do you need to be more intentional in setting aside time for your desires? Do you need to break the goal down into smaller steps? Be kind to yourself as you process.

The Nos: What do you think prevented you? (Be as specific and honest as possible.)

Were there influences outside of your control? Were you resistant/how? Do you want to focus on this goal next month, or start a new one? All responses provide opportunities for growth.

Head to next month's intentions journal page (p.158) and write the goals and alchemy you will focus on for the next 30 days.

Month No. 5 Your Free Space

Create space for your dreams to materialize. As you journey, journal here about feelings, ideas, and next steps.

"I" Statements

Write positive and empowering messages.

Month No. 6

Manifesting a Whole Perspective

Meditation takes you beyond the mind's noisy chatter into the pure awareness that is the source of all your happiness, inspiration, and love.

- DEEPAK CHOPRA, M.D.

{ finds joy in alternative medicine }

Congratulations! You have reached the halfway point traversing through the enchanted forest on the circular path towards your true self and arrived at mile-marker No. 6. Your travel bag includes the healing concepts of joy and intention, a golden feather pen, a magical magnifying glass, sage, palo santo, a clear and joyful home, and a mirror with special powers. You have assembled your life vision too. At the end of this month, you will have been following your joy for 26 weeks and focusing on your heart's desires for six months. How are you feeling? Take time to rest, rejuvenate, and honor yourself.

You are on the path at a juncture where the River of Dreams converges with the Stream of Joy and becomes the River of Authenticity. Besides the soothing babble of the water, you begin to hear the whisper of peaceful music. As you approach this month's lantern No. 6, you see a beautiful prayer rug and a heart-shaped string of gems placed on the rug. Enchanting flute sounds float through the air. You put down your travel bag, and sit on the rug in a comfortable meditative pose, relax into your body, and pick up the gemstones. You are a bit mystified as these beads, by touch alone, make you feel complete. What you thought felt like emptiness inside all of a sudden feels full. What was it you thought was missing? Place your hand over your heart and honor your entirety. What you are searching for is already part of you.

The suggested exercise for the sixth month is restorative and two-fold. I propose you find an intentional piece of jewelry, preferably made of gemstone beads, that speaks to your heart's desires, and create a meditation practice with the prayer beads that incorporates your intentions. This form of meditation is referred to as Japa and aids your sense of wholeness.

This month's color is a combination of blue and indigo. It relates to two upper spiritual chakras, Vishuddi and Ajna, the fifth and sixth energy centers located at your throat and brow. The fifth chakra has a purpose of communication and the sixth chakra a purpose of intuition and higher wisdom. Your communication, intuition, and higher wisdom are strengthened when you meditate. "I listen" is a statement.

You should sit in meditation for 20 minutes a day, unless you are too busy; then you should sit for an hour.

— ZEN PROVERB

THE SUPPORTIVE ENERGY OF MALA PRAYER BEADS

Similar to rosary beads designed to count the component prayers, a mala is a string of beads that can be used in meditation to count mantras, prayers, or breaths. A full mala contains 108 counting beads, plus one guru bead. The larger guru bead symbolizes a transformation from darkness to light. It marks the starting and ending point of the mala. A truly authentic mala is made with one continuous piece of string, and the tassel is connected to the end of the guru bead to finish the mala with a final knot. The number 108 has a powerful significance in the wholeness of existence. In the Universe, the diameter of the sun is 108 times the diameter of Earth. There are 108 letters in the Sanskrit alphabet, 108 holy sites in India, and 108 energy lines throughout the body that all converge at the heart chakra. [14]

No matter the number of beads or the design components, the true essence of intentional mala jewelry is symbolic. It is a tangible item that represents a desire, filled with an energy that you can utilize to further connect to your powerful heart. The spiritual energy held in the jewelry supports your sense of completeness. Malas are often named to honor their purpose. A name allows you to more easily connect to your expression of desire, which aids your healing process, and will help you anchor to your true self. When you aren't wearing your jewelry, place it in a special place in your home, such as your nightstand or home altar. Your beads can serve as a visual reminder of what you want to feel more of in your life and to keep your mind focused on your heart.

You've always had the power my dear,
you just had to learn it for yourself.

- GLINDA THE GOOD WITCH
{ finds joy in magic }

The concept of intentional jewelry is similar to the tale of the *Wizard of Oz*. The Wizard did not give anything to the Tin Man, Cowardly Lion, or Scarecrow that they didn't already have within themselves. A mala leads you on a journey to rediscover the power inside yourself - a mala is a reminder of what your true self already knows.

THE SUPPORTIVE ENERGY OF MANTRAS AND JAPA MEDITATION

"What is a mantra? Mantra is two words: Man and tra. Man means mind. Tra means the heat of life. Ra means sun. So, mantra is a powerful combination of words which, if recited, takes the vibratory effect of each of your molecules into the infinity of the Cosmos. That is called Mantra."

- YOGI BHAJAN
{ found joy in spirituality }

A mantra, as referenced in Yogi Bhajan's quote, translates to an instrument of the mind. Mantras are part of the 6th limb of yoga, Dharana, known as concentration. A repeated mantra helps keep you in the present moment, focusing on a positive thought. The power of the mantra is in the vibration that is created through the ritual. Remember you are communicating with God/the Universe at all times. A mantra is an affirmation expressing your desire. Your mantra can be whatever word or series of words feels right for you. For your meditation practice you could create a mantra with your keyword, a phrase that supports your intentions, or select a Sanskrit mantra such as Aham Prema (I Am Divine Love) or Om Shanti Om (Om, Dynamic Peace, Om). I frequently reference *You Can Heal Your Life* by Louise Hay for healing mantras. It is an insightful book for understanding the energetic mental patterns of disease. Louise Hay offers positive affirmations to shift your thoughts towards self-healing.

Japa is the meditative repetition of a mantra or intentional thought while utilizing a mala to count the chant. The Sanskrit word Japa translated to English means to mutter. The mantra or intention can be spoken aloud or within your mind. The meditation is generally performed sitting but can also be done standing or walking. As with all meditation styles, Japa benefits include lower blood pressure, reduced anxiety, improved sleep, increased focus, and a deeper sense of self-realization. The silence of meditation, in any form, is a heart-centered path to access your intuition at a profound level.

How I Have Found Support in a Mala and Japa Meditation

I purchased my first set of mala beads the day I graduated from the Healing Touch Energy Medicine Program. I found them at an artist co-op in Asheville, North Carolina. I had no prior knowledge about this jewelry piece I was acquiring to celebrate a long-awaited day, except that my roommate during the final training weekend wore a string of 108 gemstones. I thought the necklace looked like a fashionable accessory someone on a spiritual journey ought to wear. What surprised me instantly was how the mala made me feel when I wore it. I researched the meaning behind the stones and found they carried the energy of compassion, peace, and comfort —the same energy I felt when in contact with the mala. It was during this time that my artist dates had me returning to the bead store, and beginning to make jewelry again. For the first time, I became aware that I was sensing the energetic meanings of the gemstones and selecting them for reasons beyond their aesthetics. I found the gemstone energy to be magically heart filling. Creating a mala felt like the perfect blend of my true self-expression: jewelry + energy + intention.

Shortly after discovering a mala, I set two intentions: one for love, and one for abundance to create space for Flourish Integral Health in my life full-time. I modeled my meditation ritual based on the "40-Day Love Ritual" and the "Money Magnet Ritual," written by Heather Askinoise and Timmi Jandro in *Crystal Muse, Everyday Rituals to Tune into the Real You.* [15] I created a Love mala and an Abundance mala. I meditated around one intention in the morning and the other in the evening for 40 days. What appeared? A transformation in self-love, and a new loving partner who mirrored many healing attributes. Moreover, he helped me examine the meaning of true love, something I specifically set the intention to understand. As for my job, in meditation, I saw a runway lit with bright golden lights on either side. I knew it was a sign that it was ok to take a leap of faith, leave my corporate job, and do Flourish full-time. I kept a synchronicity journal during these 40 days, and each day was full of much abundance. Recently I have been meditating with a Truth mala. I have found truth and its healing power at a deeper level than I understood prior. I believe rituals work because you are routinely spending time thinking about, and becoming more aware of the degrees of your intentions. You are creating an environment in which you are asking for - and wide open to - guidance from God/the Universe. As stated in the World English Bible verse 7:7: "Ask, and it shall be given you: seek, and you shall find: knock, and it shall be opened to you."

HOW TO MEDITATE WITH A MALA

To use a mala in meditation, first, place your mala in your right hand. Then, place the mala over your middle finger, and use your thumb to move the beads towards you. In the yogic tradition, the index finger represents the individual soul, and the thumb represents the universal soul. The union of the two symbolizes knowledge. [16] Start at the guru bead- if your mala includes one, and connect to the intention of the mala. Then repeat your mantra, count your breath, or stay silent as you touch each of the beads, spinning each bead towards you. When you find your mind wandering, bring your thoughts back to your mantra, breath, or your inner stillness. Continue until you go full circle, reaching the guru bead or end of the mala. The meditative process of touching and spinning the beads as you focus inward directs your point of awareness to your wise heart and you become a channel of truth.

Prayer beads are a tool and Japa meditation is a practice - both help you cultivate clear inner communication. The knowledge gained from these gifts directs you towards your truth.

Week No. 23 *Your Joy*

Cultivate joy! | Begin a new tradition with family and/or friends!

Record moments of joy each day | What was your joy? Who/What gave rise to the joy? What did it feel, look, taste, smell, or sound like?

The process of reflective writing supports awareness. Awareness of what brings you joy serves as a heart-centered, resourceful compass, and unfolds more joy. The key to the journey is recognizing, understanding, and following -- your personal joy.

Joy Date · Write about your joy date - what you explored and how you felt.

Sunday _____

Monday _____

Tuesday _____

Wednesday _____

Thursday _____

Friday _____

Saturday _____

Week In Review

What was your most joyful moment this week? What themes, new or already noted, did you find in your joy moments?

The subjects have a wonderful story to tell you. And if you follow the essence -- more joy and purpose will come to light. Keep exploring your joy and add discoveries to your joy library.

Was any of your joy this week the product of working through fear and lessening your resistance towards a goal?

Recall scenarios where working through fear to reach a goal resulted in tremendous joy. With this awareness, in fearful moments you will find courage to move forward.

What were your achievements this week? Did you gain any new insights?

Note your most successful accomplishments, quality time with loved ones, and enlightening moments. Flip back periodically to honor your attentiveness to your priorities and review what you have learned.

Did you face challenges this week? Do you see different possibilities? How will you adjust moving forward?

Learning happens when you reflect and make adjustments to your course. Your growth is the product of working through struggles and finding a heart-centered solution. Joy resides here, too!

What kindness did you extend? How did you feel during and afterward?

Noting the kindness you extend during the week helps you to honor your light and love yourself more.

Use this space to begin planning for more joy in your life.

Dedicating time for joy makes your days brighter and more meaningful.

People

Places

Things

Experiences

Joy Date Ideas

Week No. 24 *Your Joy*

Cultivate joy! | Spend time with someone who inspires you!

Record moments of joy each day | What was your joy? Who/What gave rise to the joy? What did it feel, look, taste, smell, or sound like?

The process of reflective writing supports awareness. Awareness of what brings you joy serves as a heart-centered, resourceful compass, and unfolds more joy. The key to the journey is recognizing, understanding, and following -- your personal joy.

Joy Date · Write about your joy date - what you explored and how you felt.

_____

Sunday _____

_____

Monday _____

_____

Tuesday _____

_____

Wednesday _____

_____

Thursday _____

_____

Friday _____

_____

Saturday _____

_____

Week In Review

What was your most joyful moment this week? What themes, new or already noted, did you find in your joy moments?

The subjects have a wonderful story to tell you. And if you follow the essence -- more joy and purpose will come to light. Keep exploring your joy and add discoveries to your joy library.

Was any of your joy this week the product of working through fear and lessening your resistance towards a goal?

Recall scenarios where working through fear to reach a goal resulted in tremendous joy. With this awareness, in fearful moments you will find courage to move forward.

What were your achievements this week? Did you gain any new insights?

Note your most successful accomplishments, quality time with loved ones, and enlightening moments. Flip back periodically to honor your attentiveness to your priorities and review what you have learned.

Did you face challenges this week? Do you see different possibilities? How will you adjust moving forward?

Learning happens when you reflect and make adjustments to your course. Your growth is the product of working through struggles and finding a heart-centered solution. Joy resides here, too!

What kindness did you extend? How did you feel during and afterward?

Noting the kindness you extend during the week helps you to honor your light and love yourself more.

Use this space to begin planning for more joy in your life.

Dedicating time for joy makes your days brighter and more meaningful.

People

Places

Things

Experiences

Joy Date Ideas

Week No. 25 *Your Joy*

Cultivate joy! | Really listen. Don't interrupt!

Record moments of joy each day

What was your joy? Who/What gave rise to the joy? What did it feel, look, taste, smell, or sound like?

The process of reflective writing supports awareness. Awareness of what brings you joy serves as a heart-centered, resourceful compass, and unfolds more joy. The key to the journey is recognizing, understanding, and following -- your personal joy.

Joy Date · Write about your joy date - what you explored and how you felt.

Sunday _____

Monday _____

Tuesday _____

Wednesday _____

Thursday _____

Friday _____

Saturday _____

Week In Review

What was your most joyful moment this week? What themes, new or already noted, did you find in your joy moments?

The subjects have a wonderful story to tell you. And if you follow the essence -- more joy and purpose will come to light. Keep exploring your joy and add discoveries to your joy library.

Scatter joy!
- RALPH WALDO EMERSON
{ found joy in poetry }

Was any of your joy this week the product of working through fear and lessening your resistance towards a goal?

Recall scenarios where working through fear to reach a goal resulted in tremendous joy. With this awareness, in fearful moments you will find courage to move forward.

What were your achievements this week? Did you gain any new insights?

Note your most successful accomplishments, quality time with loved ones, and enlightening moments. Flip back periodically to honor your attentiveness to your priorities and review what you have learned.

Did you face challenges this week? Do you see different possibilities? How will you adjust moving forward?

Learning happens when you reflect and make adjustments to your course. Your growth is the product of working through struggles and finding a heart-centered solution. Joy resides here, too!

What kindness did you extend? How did you feel during and afterward?

Noting the kindness you extend during the week helps you to honor your light and love yourself more.

Use this space to begin planning for more joy in your life.

Dedicating time for joy makes your days brighter and more meaningful.

People
Places
Things
Experiences
Joy Date Ideas

Week No. 26 *Your Joy*

Cultivate joy! | Write ten things that inspire gratitude!

Record moments of joy each day | What was your joy? Who/What gave rise to the joy? What did it feel, look, taste, smell, or sound like?

The process of reflective writing supports awareness. Awareness of what brings you joy serves as a heart-centered, resourceful compass, and unfolds more joy. The key to the journey is recognizing, understanding, and following -- your personal joy.

Joy Date · Write about your joy date - what you explored and how you felt.

Sunday _____

Monday _____

Tuesday _____

Wednesday _____

Thursday _____

Friday _____

Saturday _____

Week In Review

What was your most joyful moment this week? What themes, new or already noted, did you find in your joy moments?

The subjects have a wonderful story to tell you. And if you follow the essence -- more joy and purpose will come to light. Keep exploring your joy and add discoveries to your joy library.

Was any of your joy this week the product of working through fear and lessening your resistance towards a goal?

Recall scenarios where working through fear to reach a goal resulted in tremendous joy. With this awareness, in fearful moments you will find courage to move forward.

What were your achievements this week? Did you gain any new insights?

Note your most successful accomplishments, quality time with loved ones, and enlightening moments. Flip back periodically to honor your attentiveness to your priorities and review what you have learned.

Did you face challenges this week? Do you see different possibilities? How will you adjust moving forward?

Learning happens when you reflect and make adjustments to your course. Your growth is the product of working through struggles and finding a heart-centered solution. Joy resides here, too!

What kindness did you extend? How did you feel during and afterward?

Noting the kindness you extend during the week helps you to honor your light and love yourself more.

Use this space to begin planning for more joy in your life.

Dedicating time for joy makes your days brighter and more meaningful.

People

Places

Things

Experiences

Joy Date Ideas

Month No. 6 *Your Intentions*

YOUR KEYWORD

Along with your keyword, draw on the inner strength of curiosity, hope, and self-compassion as you approach your intentions.

Track the energy that you put towards your aspirations, and observe what is gained. Remember that being intentional about how you spend your time will help you achieve your goals. Where your attention goes, your energy flows.

No. 01

DESIRED GOAL:

ALCHEMY:

1	2	3	4	5	6	7
8	9	10	11	12	13	14
15	16	17	18	19	20	21
22	23	24	25	26	27	28
29	30	31				

No. 02

DESIRED GOAL:

ALCHEMY:

1	2	3	4	5	6	7
8	9	10	11	12	13	14
15	16	17	18	19	20	21
22	23	24	25	26	27	28
29	30	31				

No. 03

DESIRED GOAL:

ALCHEMY:

1	2	3	4	5	6	7
8	9	10	11	12	13	14
15	16	17	18	19	20	21
22	23	24	25	26	27	28
29	30	31				

No. 04

DESIRED GOAL:

ALCHEMY:

1	2	3	4	5	6	7
8	9	10	11	12	13	14
15	16	17	18	19	20	21
22	23	24	25	26	27	28
29	30	31				

Month In Review

Reflect on your time spent working towards your intentions.
Did you spend time as planned on your goals? Have you released what you needed to, and started to refine your focus? Record below a yes, partial, or no.

GOAL/ALCHEMY No. 01

GOAL/ALCHEMY No. 02

GOAL/ALCHEMY No. 03

GOAL/ALCHEMY No. 04

When a person really desires something, all the universe conspires to help that person to realize his dream.

- PAULO COELHO

{ finds joy in writing }

The yesses: Congratulations! Write about your successes.
How do you feel? What does this accomplishment offer you? If you no longer need to track this goal, consider introducing a new intention from your Month No. 1 exercise.

The partials: Is there anything new that you could implement that would help you achieve your goals?
Do you need to be more intentional in setting aside time for your desires? Do you need to break the goal down into smaller steps? Be kind to yourself as you process.

The Nos: What do you think prevented you? (Be as specific and honest as possible.)
Were there influences outside of your control? Were you resistant/how? Do you want to focus on this goal next month, or start a new one? All responses provide opportunities for growth.

Head to next month's intentions journal page (p.182) and write the goals and alchemy you will focus on for the next 30 days.

Month No. 6 *Your Free Space*

Create space for your dreams to materialize. As you journey, journal here about feelings, ideas, and next steps.

"I" Statements

Write positive and empowering messages.

Love
Eternity

Water Rest Area
Picnic Rest Area
Vista Rest Area

Picnic Rest Area *Your Midpoint Celebration*

The more you celebrate your life,
the more there is in life to celebrate.

- OPRAH WINFREY

{ finds joy in purpose }

Deeper into the forest, and towards the end of another full day of adventure, you arrive upon a most magical setting. Strings of small warm globe lights hang from the tree branches to create a chandelier above a perfectly sized table. The day's soft flute music transitions to the sounds of a rich jazz trio, and a comforting voice is singing the "Nearness of You." (In my dream this is James Taylor's voice.) As you walk closer towards the white linen-covered table, you see a stylishly curated vintage silver, china, and crystal set. The forest has created a fairy tale evening featuring your favorite dishes as a way to celebrate the midway point of your journey. You sit down in a velvet paneled chair and savor each morsel and minute of this thoughtfully and generously provided experience.

Many years ago, I experienced a joyful hiking moment walking a trail near Bozeman, Montana that partially inspired this rest stop. At a rest period, our trail guide charmingly appeared with a silver tray full of delightful snacks, each decorated with colorful toothpick umbrellas. A simple, yet exceptionally bright moment that remains in my memory. Before continuing onto the second half of the path, I encourage you to rest. *Celebrate you and your journey*. For your inspiration, included are three *celebratory* (not all healthy!) recipes.

You might find this cookbook page unusual for personal growth reading. The design format of *Flourish* is inspired by *Elements of Style: Designing a Home & a Life* by Erin Gates. Recipes are included in the kitchen chapter. Now you have the connection and second part of my inspiration. Enjoy!

Tomato Crostini with Whipped Feta

6 ounces good feta cheese, crumbled

2 ounces cream cheese, at room temperature

⅔ cup good olive oil, divided

2 Tbsp. freshly squeezed lemon juice

Kosher salt and freshly ground

2 Tbsp. pine nuts

2 Tbsp. minced shallots (2 shallots)

2 tsp. minced garlic (2 cloves)

2 Tbsp. good red wine vinegar

2 pounds ripe heirloom tomatoes, ½" diced

3 Tbsp. julienned fresh basil leaves, plus extra for serving

20 to 25 (½" thick) diagonal baguette slices

Place feta and cream cheese in the bowl of a food processor fitted with a steel blade. Pulse until cheeses are mixed. Add ⅓ cup olive oil, lemon juice, ½ tsp salt, and ¼ tsp. pepper and process until smooth. Refrigerate until ready to serve.

Place pine nuts in a dry saute pan over low heat and cook for 5 to 10 minutes, stirring often, until lightly browned. Set aside.

For the tomato topping, up to an hour before serving, combine shallots, garlic, and vinegar in a medium bowl. Set aside 5 minutes to allow shallots to absorb vinegar. Whisk in remaining ⅓ cup olive oil, 1 tsp. salt, ½ tsp. pepper. Add tomatoes, stir gently, and set aside for 10 minutes. Stir in basil and taste for seasoning.

Place the bread slices, lightly brushed with olive oil in a 425 degree oven and bake for 6 to 8 minutes until lightly browned. Remove from the oven and let cool on a wire rack.

Generously spread whipped feta on each bread slice. With a slotted spoon, place tomatoes on top. Put crostini on plates and scatter with the reserved toasted pine nuts. Sprinkle with basil and serve. Makes 20 to 25 Crostini. [17]

Creamy Crab Dip

½ cup sour cream

½ cup mayo

3 oz. cream cheese

1 teaspoon worcheshire

¼ teaspoon Lawry's seasoned salt

1 tablespoon lemon juice

3 to 4 drops hot sauce

6 oz refrigerated high quality crab meat, drained and flaked

Mix all ingredients, and refrigerate 3 to 4 hours before serving. [18] Serve with Fritos dippers, or crackers.

Grandma McCabe's* Sour Cream Cupcakes

Preheat oven to 375 degrees

Mix 2 eggs and 1 cup light brown sugar

Add, 1 cup sour cream

¼ teaspoon almond extract

½ teaspoon vanilla extract

Mix, and then add and mix

1 ½ cup sifted flour

1 teaspoon baking soda

¼ teaspoon salt

Makes about one dozen cupcakes. Pour batter into cupcake liners and bake for approximately 18 minutes. Pay attention as they bake, to avoid overbaking. *Since childhood I have thought of this recipe as my Grandma's. While working on this book I learned the source is unknown. This recipe was refreshed from the original version for *Flourish*. Over time the ingredient's composition changed, therefore changing the final cupcake.

Frosting

Mix 3 tablespoons of softened butter and 2 cups of confectioners sugar. Then add, 2 tablespoon of 2% milk and 1 ½ teaspoons of vanilla extract.

Love

Eternity

💧 Water Rest Area

🪑 Picnic Rest Area

🏔 Vista Rest Area

Month No. 7

Journaling to Connect

I write entirely to find out what I am thinking, what I am looking at,
what I see and what it means, what I want and what I fear.

- JOAN DIDION

{ found joy in writing }

Your meditation rug is rolled up and attached to your travel bag. Your mala beads are in your pocket, around your wrist, or around your neck, laying against your chest. Your magical healing tools feel light. Excited about your future, you are walking at a pace perfect for you towards mile-marker No. 7. You reflect on how you are alone in the silence of the forest, yet this singularity does not make you sad. You feel stronger each day of the journey. You are cultivating your inner-fortitude.

As you approach lantern No. 7, you see another gift. A golden notebook, with your name and phone number written on the inside cover – in case you lose it, is shining brightly on the path. This forest seems to know everything about you. You rest your travel bag down on the path. You pick up the notebook, and sit with your back up against a tree. You pull out your magical golden feather pen, open the first page of the light-filled journal, and begin writing about your day's adventure. Words flow as you describe what brought you joy and what brought you heartache. What quickly catches your attention is the sense of clarity and lightness you experience as you write about your thoughts and feelings. You have added another gem to your healing toolkit.

Blue is the color of your throat chakra. This chakra's purpose is to express, and it embodies the affirmation, "I speak." This month you will connect to your voice.

Putting pen to paper, or fingers to the electronic device, and translating your inner world into physical reality is cathartic. The action of writing helps restore wholeness as your thoughts and feelings are no longer isolated. Processing your senses into written words blends your inner reality and your outer reality. To further support listening to your wise heart, the intention for the seventh month is for you to create a journaling practice. If you already journal, consider incorporating a new theme.

THE MAGIC OF JOURNALING

Because being a CEO can feel lonely, I journal religiously as a way to express my thoughts, feelings and aspirations. Looking back at earlier entries helps me reflect on challenges and celebrate progress and successes.

- RANA EL KALIOUBY

{ finds joy in expression recognition }

Journaling is an effective means to process your life and find answers within. Writing can help to slow down your thoughts, and foster a deeper level of honesty with yourself. The process can help you to "get to the truth faster," as mentioned by Kathleen Adams in *Journal to Self*. [19] The writing process helps you identify what to release and make enlightening connections that can be challenging to link solely in your mind. A journal can feel like a trusted friend, helping you become more lovingly aware of what is taking place inside you. Writing can also help you gain confidence and clarity to better speak your truth. The writing process can be one of great self-discovery and transformation towards your dreams.

JOURNAL TIPS AND THEME SUGGESTIONS

1. Journal in a notebook that feels inspiring, the right size for you, and comfortable to write in. Treat yourself to a little luxury!

2. Make the process fun with colorful pens (I love Le Pen and Tombow pens) and accessories, like washi tape, a joyful ruler, and sticky divider tabs.

3. Create a routine time of day to reflect in your journal. The process may become a part of your day that you look forward to.

A theme, or prompt, can help if you are new to journaling. Here are some suggestions:

* Synchronicity Journaling - Do you ever experience days where everything seems to fall into place? Keep notes about the magical coincidences in your life. How do they make you feel? This practice helps you hone your intuition, and see the hidden meanings around you.

* Dream Journaling - Keep a journal by your bed and write about your dreams the moment that you wake up. Most likely, you will begin to make connections and find symbolism within your dreams. This can help you navigate your life more intuitively. You might find yourself solving problems in your dreams.

* Meditation Journaling - Write what you sense in your meditations. Similar to a dream journal, this process will help you link your inner life with your physical reality. You can also examine the relationship between your meditations and your intentions.

* Expressive Journaling - When you are upset, write about what is bothering you in whatever penmanship you need at that moment. Writing about the source of your stress can help you find the root cause and let go. Journaling can also help you discern opportunities to heal and grow. Pulling out your expressive pages and disposing of them (or burning them) can also help release energy.

* The Artist's Way Morning Pages Journaling- Write three full pages each morning. Journal about whatever is on your mind. You might discover that you write about the same thing every morning. Over time, taking time to sit down and write will help you gain clarity which will then lead to action.

* Sleepless Night Journaling - When your mind is spinning, turn on the light and write the reasons why you are still awake. List your fears, and the things you are thinking about for the future. Once you've put your thoughts on paper, you most likely will find it easier to fall back asleep. Write on paper with a night light so that the blue light of your device doesn't cause you to produce cortisol and impede the "going back to sleep" process.

* Bullet Journal - Bullet journaling is a method created by Ryder Carroll to keep everything in your mind organized. There are endless resources online for anyone who wants to start bullet journaling, from suggestions for first spreads to what style notebook to purchase. A bullet journal starts as a book of blank pages, and you create a custom tool to support one or multiple aspects of your life.

How I Find Journaling Transformative

The Artist's Way morning pages were the impetus of my writing habit. I found the experience to be a mind cleanse. In addition to helping me release, I discovered that writing helped me better understand how I could change. Moreover, writing helped me garner the courage to do so. I continued to write morning pages for several years because the process was so supportive. Soon after starting *The Artist's Way,* I began writing about joy too. More recently, I started a journaling practice to support my work hours. I begin the day by writing a few affirmations, followed by bullet-pointing my daily goals on the right-side pages (I love Franklin-Covey tracking methods). When I get to the end of a given notebook, I turn around and write in reverse on the left side pages. I find this writing method inspiring. Looking back on my past journal entries helps pay tribute to the progress of creating, and cultivates faith, including that *everything does work out in the end.*

Some journals might feel best released, and others are worthy keepsakes. Reading through old journal pages can be similar to looking at old photographs and cards from loved ones. They help tell your life's story. When you revisit your journals in the future, you can honor your past and see yourself in a new light. Journaling is a creative process that ultimately empowers you to understand yourself and to be your true self.

All you have to do is write one true sentence.
Write the truest sentence that you know.

- ERNEST HEMINGWAY

{ found joy in writing }

Week No. 27 *Your Joy*

Cultivate joy! | Write a positive online review of a business you appreciate!

Record moments of joy each day | What was your joy? Who/What gave rise to the joy? What did it feel, look, taste, smell, or sound like?

The process of reflective writing supports awareness. Awareness of what brings you joy serves as a heart-centered, resourceful compass, and unfolds more joy. The key to the journey is recognizing, understanding, and following -- your personal joy.

Joy Date · Write about your joy date - what you explored and how you felt.

_____

Sunday _____

_____

Monday _____

_____

Tuesday _____

_____

Wednesday _____

_____

Thursday _____

_____

Friday _____

_____

Saturday _____

_____

Week In Review

What was your most joyful moment this week? What themes, new or already noted, did you find in your joy moments?

The subjects have a wonderful story to tell you. And if you follow the essence -- more joy and purpose will come to light. Keep exploring your joy and add discoveries to your joy library.

Was any of your joy this week the product of working through fear and lessening your resistance towards a goal?

Recall scenarios where working through fear to reach a goal resulted in tremendous joy. With this awareness, in fearful moments you will find courage to move forward.

What were your achievements this week? Did you gain any new insights?

Note your most successful accomplishments, quality time with loved ones, and enlightening moments. Flip back periodically to honor your attentiveness to your priorities and review what you have learned.

Did you face challenges this week? Do you see different possibilities? How will you adjust moving forward?

Learning happens when you reflect and make adjustments to your course. Your growth is the product of working through struggles and finding a heart-centered solution. Joy resides here, too!

What kindness did you extend? How did you feel during and afterward?

Noting the kindness you extend during the week helps you to honor your light and love yourself more.

Use this space to begin planning for more joy in your life.

Dedicating time for joy makes your days brighter and more meaningful.

People

Places

Things

Experiences

Joy Date Ideas

Week No. 28 *Your Joy*

Cultivate joy! | Go on a day trip adventure!

Record moments of joy each day

What was your joy? Who/What gave rise to the joy? What did it feel, look, taste, smell, or sound like?

The process of reflective writing supports awareness. Awareness of what brings you joy serves as a heart-centered, resourceful compass, and unfolds more joy. The key to the journey is recognizing, understanding, and following -- your personal joy.

Joy Date · Write about your joy date - what you explored and how you felt.

Sunday _____

Monday _____

Tuesday _____

Wednesday _____

Thursday _____

Friday _____

Saturday _____

Week In Review

What was your most joyful moment this week? What themes, new or already noted, did you find in your joy moments?

The subjects have a wonderful story to tell you. And if you follow the essence -- more joy and purpose will come to light. Keep exploring your joy and add discoveries to your joy library.

If you carry joy in your heart, you can heal any moment.
- CARLOS SANTANA
{ finds joy in music }

Was any of your joy this week the product of working through fear and lessening your resistance towards a goal?

Recall scenarios where working through fear to reach a goal resulted in tremendous joy. With this awareness, in fearful moments you will find courage to move forward.

What were your achievements this week? Did you gain any new insights?

Note your most successful accomplishments, quality time with loved ones, and enlightening moments. Flip back periodically to honor your attentiveness to your priorities and review what you have learned.

Did you face challenges this week? Do you see different possibilities? How will you adjust moving forward?

Learning happens when you reflect and make adjustments to your course. Your growth is the product of working through struggles and finding a heart-centered solution. Joy resides here, too!

What kindness did you extend? How did you feel during and afterward?

Noting the kindness you extend during the week helps you to honor your light and love yourself more.

Use this space to begin planning for more joy in your life.

Dedicating time for joy makes your days brighter and more meaningful.

People

Places

Things

Experiences

Joy Date Ideas

Week No. 29 *Your Joy*

Cultivate joy! | Ask someone about their formula for happiness!

Record moments of joy each day | What was your joy? Who/What gave rise to the joy? What did it feel, look, taste, smell, or sound like?

The process of reflective writing supports awareness. Awareness of what brings you joy serves as a heart-centered, resourceful compass, and unfolds more joy. The key to the journey is recognizing, understanding, and following -- your personal joy.

Joy Date · Write about your joy date - what you explored and how you felt.

Sunday _____

Monday _____

Tuesday _____

Wednesday _____

Thursday _____

Friday _____

Saturday _____

Week In Review

What was your most joyful moment this week? What themes, new or already noted, did you find in your joy moments?

The subjects have a wonderful story to tell you. And if you follow the essence -- more joy and purpose will come to light. Keep exploring your joy and add discoveries to your joy library.

Was any of your joy this week the product of working through fear and lessening your resistance towards a goal?

Recall scenarios where working through fear to reach a goal resulted in tremendous joy. With this awareness, in fearful moments you will find courage to move forward.

What were your achievements this week? Did you gain any new insights?

Note your most successful accomplishments, quality time with loved ones, and enlightening moments. Flip back periodically to honor your attentiveness to your priorities and review what you have learned.

Did you face challenges this week? Do you see different possibilities? How will you adjust moving forward?

Learning happens when you reflect and make adjustments to your course. Your growth is the product of working through struggles and finding a heart-centered solution. Joy resides here, too!

What kindness did you extend? How did you feel during and afterward?

Noting the kindness you extend during the week helps you to honor your light and love yourself more.

Use this space to begin planning for more joy in your life.

Dedicating time for joy makes your days brighter and more meaningful.

People

Places

Things

Experiences

Joy Date Ideas

Week No. 30 *Your Joy*

Cultivate joy! | Feeling gloomy? Buy yourself a fun card and a bright plant.

Record moments of joy each day

What was your joy? Who/What gave rise to the joy? What did it feel, look, taste, smell, or sound like?

The process of reflective writing supports awareness. Awareness of what brings you joy serves as a heart-centered, resourceful compass, and unfolds more joy. The key to the journey is recognizing, understanding, and following -- your personal joy.

Joy Date · Write about your joy date - what you explored and how you felt.

_____

Sunday _____

Monday _____

Tuesday _____

Wednesday _____

Thursday _____

Friday _____

Saturday _____

Week In Review

What was your most joyful moment this week? What themes, new or already noted, did you find in your joy moments?

The subjects have a wonderful story to tell you. And if you follow the essence -- more joy and purpose will come to light. Keep exploring your joy and add discoveries to your joy library.

Was any of your joy this week the product of working through fear and lessening your resistance towards a goal?

Recall scenarios where working through fear to reach a goal resulted in tremendous joy. With this awareness, in fearful moments you will find courage to move forward.

What were your achievements this week? Did you gain any new insights?

Note your most successful accomplishments, quality time with loved ones, and enlightening moments. Flip back periodically to honor your attentiveness to your priorities and review what you have learned.

Did you face challenges this week? Do you see different possibilities? How will you adjust moving forward?

Learning happens when you reflect and make adjustments to your course. Your growth is the product of working through struggles and finding a heart-centered solution. Joy resides here, too!

What kindness did you extend? How did you feel during and afterward?

Noting the kindness you extend during the week helps you to honor your light and love yourself more.

Use this space to begin planning for more joy in your life.

Dedicating time for joy makes your days brighter and more meaningful.

People

Places

Things

Experiences

Joy Date Ideas

Week No. 31 *Your Joy*

Cultivate joy! | Make a helpful introduction!

Record moments of joy each day

What was your joy? Who/What gave rise to the joy? What did it feel, look, taste, smell, or sound like?

The process of reflective writing supports awareness. Awareness of what brings you joy serves as a heart-centered, resourceful compass, and unfolds more joy. The key to the journey is recognizing, understanding, and following -- your personal joy.

Joy Date · Write about your joy date - what you explored and how you felt.

Sunday _____

Monday _____

Tuesday _____

Wednesday _____

Thursday _____

Friday _____

Saturday _____

Week In Review

What was your most joyful moment this week? What themes, new or already noted, did you find in your joy moments?

The subjects have a wonderful story to tell you. And if you follow the essence -- more joy and purpose will come to light. Keep exploring your joy and add discoveries to your joy library.

Was any of your joy this week the product of working through fear and lessening your resistance towards a goal?

Recall scenarios where working through fear to reach a goal resulted in tremendous joy. With this awareness, in fearful moments you will find courage to move forward.

What were your achievements this week? Did you gain any new insights?

Note your most successful accomplishments, quality time with loved ones, and enlightening moments. Flip back periodically to honor your attentiveness to your priorities and review what you have learned.

Did you face challenges this week? Do you see different possibilities? How will you adjust moving forward?

Learning happens when you reflect and make adjustments to your course. Your growth is the product of working through struggles and finding a heart-centered solution. Joy resides here, too!

What kindness did you extend? How did you feel during and afterward?

Noting the kindness you extend during the week helps you to honor your light and love yourself more.

Use this space to begin planning for more joy in your life.

Dedicating time for joy makes your days brighter and more meaningful.

People

Places

Things

Experiences

Joy Date Ideas

Your Intentions

YOUR KEYWORD

Along with your keyword, draw on the inner strength of curiosity, hope, and self-compassion as you approach your intentions.

Track the energy that you put towards your aspirations, and observe what is gained. Remember that being intentional about how you spend your time will help you achieve your goals. Where your attention goes, your energy flows.

No. 01

DESIRED GOAL:

ALCHEMY:

1	2	3	4	5	6	7
8	9	10	11	12	13	14
15	16	17	18	19	20	21
22	23	24	25	26	27	28
29	30	31				

No. 02

DESIRED GOAL:

ALCHEMY:

1	2	3	4	5	6	7
8	9	10	11	12	13	14
15	16	17	18	19	20	21
22	23	24	25	26	27	28
29	30	31				

No. 03

DESIRED GOAL:

ALCHEMY:

1	2	3	4	5	6	7
8	9	10	11	12	13	14
15	16	17	18	19	20	21
22	23	24	25	26	27	28
29	30	31				

No. 04

DESIRED GOAL:

ALCHEMY:

1	2	3	4	5	6	7
8	9	10	11	12	13	14
15	16	17	18	19	20	21
22	23	24	25	26	27	28
29	30	31				

Month In Review

Reflect on your time spent working towards your intentions.

Did you spend time as planned on your goals? Have you released what you needed to, and started to refine your focus? Record below a yes, partial, or no.

GOAL/ALCHEMY No. 01

GOAL/ALCHEMY No. 02

GOAL/ALCHEMY No. 03

GOAL/ALCHEMY No. 04

When you get right down to it, intentional living is about living your best story.

-JOHN C. MAXWELL

{ finds joy in leadership }

The yesses: Congratulations! Write about your successes.

How do you feel? What does this accomplishment offer you? If you no longer need to track this goal, consider introducing a new intention from your Month No. 1 exercise.

The partials: Is there anything new that you could implement that would help you achieve your goals?

Do you need to be more intentional in setting aside time for your desires? Do you need to break the goal down into smaller steps? Be kind to yourself as you process.

The Nos: What do you think prevented you? (Be as specific and honest as possible.)

Were there influences outside of your control? Were you resistant/how? Do you want to focus on this goal next month, or start a new one? All responses provide opportunities for growth.

Head to next month's intentions journal page (p.202) and write the goals and alchemy you will focus on for the next 30 days.

Month No. 7 *Your Free Space*

Create space for your dreams to materialize. As you journey, journal here about feelings, ideas, and next steps.

"I" Statements

Write positive and empowering messages.

Month No. 8

Healing with Holistic Health Care

The first wealth is health.

— RALPH WALDO EMERSON

{ found joy in poetry }

Back on the magical path, approaching lantern No. 8, you see a figure ahead; this is the first person you are encountering on the circular path. You wonder if perhaps they are on a similar journey. You strike up a conversation as you are excited to talk with another person on what has been a silent journey. It turns out, yes, they are also on an adventure to find all the love inside themselves. Their journey blends with your journey at this light post. They share that the engaging forest asked them to meet you here.

Sometimes we need support from a trusted companion. For the next hour, this confidant is going to help you release what you are working on letting go, they are going to become a channel to support your whole intentions. You roll out your meditation rug, sit down, and open your journal. You share which intention statement you are struggling with the most. This heart-centered person by your side assures you that you have everything inside yourself to create your true desires and then opens up their light-filled medicine bag in support of your dreams. Two are now gathered with a mutual goal, to see you flourish.

You have reached month eight of the *Flourish* journey. Do you feel different since you began? What does your perception of your heart's desires look like now? You have done beautiful work in defining your intentions and routinely working towards them. You've spent time creating your life's vision, facing your fears, and tidying and blessing your home. You've cultivated healthy boundaries and a supportive self-care routine. You've honed your listening and journaling to make insightful connections. I hope you are proud of yourself.

Violet-White is the color of Sahasrara, the Crown chakra. Its purpose is your utmost clarity, higher-thought, and the statement, "I know". It is the meeting point between your physical body and your eternal spiritual presence. This month you will connect to your crown chakra to align with your personal power.

For this month, the suggestion is to incorporate holistic health care into your wellness routine. If you are unfamiliar with the work, I recommend finding professionally trained practitioners and exploring various modalities to discover what feels right for you. One or two regular sessions a month can support your whole being and instill peace beyond the session. If you already work with a trusted practitioner, consider trying a different modality. Even if you only have one visit, it will open up a part of you for further exploration. While I was going through Energy Medicine training, one requirement was to experience ten different alternative healing modalities. I found the sessions enlightening and expansive.

WHAT IS HOLISTIC CARE?

Holistic medicine approaches healing by addressing all of you simultaneously - physical, mental, emotional, and spiritual. Care is based on the foundational concept that every part of you influences your whole health. Many of the modalities that fall under the umbrella of holistic health care (also referred to as complementary and alternative medicine, or CAM) are based on the principle that our bodies are comprised of energy meridians (also referred to as channels) and energy chakras. Each of the energy lines and centers relates to specific physical, emotional, mental, and spiritual aspects of your whole being. Life experiences are recorded in our energy systems. Some of these experiences present as a disease in the body. We, and all our surroundings, are energy in various vibrational forms. Disease is an energy form too. Alternative medicine balances the body's subtle energy systems to remove the energy of disease and maintain health and wellness.

Everything is energy and that's all there is to it.
Match the frequency of the reality you want and you cannot
help but get that reality. It can be no other way.
This is not philosophy. This is physics.

- ALBERT EINSTEIN

{ found joy in physics }

Holistic health care is a broad term that applies to many different modalities of various traditions. Many of the practices like Acupuncture, Ayurvedic medicine, Reiki, and Shamanic healing date back thousands of years. Each modality has a word to describe life force and a signature method of moving, balancing, and strengthening energy. Acupuncture utilizes hair-thin needles inserted in the skin at specific points to harmoniously heal a patient. A Reiki practitioner connects to pure consciousness through symbology, hand movements, and the chakra system to attune a client to a higher vibration. In addition to utilizing hand movements and whole health mental imagery to balance the energy bodies, a Healing Touch session revolves around a mutual intention statement for healing. Emotional Freedom Technique incorporates tapping and positive affirmations, along meridians, to create positive change. Each modality's action shifts the body's energy systems into a parasympathetic state and the body-mind-spirit enters an intuitive healing process. Treatments can induce a relaxation response, correct imbalances, increase blood flow, regulate hormones, and release toxins. In addition to the physical healing, the emotional, mental, and spiritual body is also positively influenced.

Your body is designed to heal itself. The ability of a
body to maintain its health and overcome illness is, in
fact, among nature's most remarkable feats.

- DONNA EDEN

{ finds joy in Energy Medicine }

APPLICATIONS

Holistic healing can be applied to many facets including relief from physical pain (such as headaches, migraines, and back pain), palliative care, cancer support, post-operative care, and reducing stress, anxiety, and depression. Complementary and alternative medicine can also be useful to help maintain wellness, strengthen the immune system, support digestive functions, and expand consciousness.

MODALITIES TO EXPLORE

There are many holistic health care modalities. They generally fall into these categories: traditional alternative medicine, body and movement, diet and herbs, energy and vibrational medicine, spiritual practices, and body-centered psychotherapy. Here is a list of modalities to consider exploring.

Acupuncture

Ayurveda

Barbara Brennan School of Healing

Body Talk

Craniosacral Therapy

Emotional Freedom Technique

Healing Touch

Massage Therapy

Psychotherapy

Reiki

Shamanic Healing

Yoga

How Holistic Medicine Has Influenced My Life

Holistic health care positively supports my life, both as a client and as a practitioner. I experienced a recurring cycle of autoimmune disease beginning in my late teens. Initially, I suffered from stage four endometriosis, then autoimmune-based infertility, followed by Epstein Barr, mono, two mystery autoimmune diseases, and IBS. For over 15 years, I worked with acupuncturists to reduce painful symptoms of endometriosis, support fertility, and strengthen my immune system. In all instances, I found relief and healing. Although the work did not lead to a pregnancy, acupuncture and Chinese herb treatments helped me heal abnormal fibrous tissue growth outside of my uterus and eliminate painful symptoms of endometriosis. The most transformative healing that I experienced could be attributed to a series of biofield healing sessions over five months, combined with homeopathic treatments. At the tail end of these treatments, what I first experienced was labeled as acute pancreatitis followed by what I now understand to be a Kundalini awakening. During my awakening I experienced a vivid dream in which I was flying above cities full of bright white lights while intense bursts of energy were running along my spine. The energy started briefly a few days prior in a meditation and remained for several days after the dream. I felt elevated and bewildered. After this awakening I became free of my autoimmune illness pattern. In addition to the physical healing, I gained emotional and mental strength.

Unfortunately, violations can happen anywhere; the holistic health care space that I find supportive also caused pain in my life. As I reached my health peak, I experienced abuse from the two practitioners who supported my healing. I never experienced suicidal ideation before this time, so I am certain that the experience led to my tipping point. How I was energetically abused is difficult to understand, and that confusion contributed to my despair. In addition to the Kundalini energy, I experienced a blissful energy in my body. My first instinct was that I was being preyed upon, however, I was led to believe that the unfamiliar sensations were a result of my healing. The healers, in time, revealed themselves as the source of the blissful energy (felt from miles away), and told me that I was part of a soul family hierarchy instilling a sense of purpose. In retrospect, cult-like, as they claimed direct access to the energy and to God/the Universe. I felt fear when I heard this information, yet I ignored my intuition. The practitioners promised that I would learn how to access the energy myself, and I chose to believe that others were more powerful than myself. The energy experienced from a distance became predatory and physically manipulative. I was unable to comprehend, and I felt consumed by a need to try and understand. Adding to my angst, also in retrospect, was an experience of gaslighting. Further, I was abused by women and that created pain in my relationship to my heterosexual identity. Walking into a new therapist's office for the first time, alone in a quiet hallway, I heard a strong unfamiliar voice that sounded outside of me confirm my truth. (I was under the care of two therapists at my darkest time, one a referral from the abusers, and treatment increased my anxiety. I was not transparent with either provider because I was too frightened to share my truth.) The resulting trauma felt in my body was most troubling, and from what I sought relief. I have worked hard to make sense of and accept the experience. I continue to work on healing the post-traumatic stress and alchemizing the energy into graceful strength and freedom.

Openly discussing abuse, trauma and even spiritual awakenings evokes fear. Feelings of shame and discomfort associated with the possibility of not being understood or believed surfaced. Part of my healing process has included educating myself. That has led to empowerment. The inclusion illuminates the path of following joy is directly related to healing from despair. Speaking up is also my sincere effort to raise awareness and help break the cycle of abuse in any form. Dr. Victor Frankl writes in *Man's Search for Meaning*, "In some way, suffering ceases to be suffering at the moment it finds meaning."

All truths are easy to understand once they are discovered;
the point is to discover them.

- GALILEO GALILEI

{ found joy in the stars }

To understand more about how energetically adept people can influence another person from a distance, I recommend watching "The Energy Experience" episode of Gwyneth Paltrow's *The Goop Lab* on Netflix. This segment illustrates energy work and how the body can react without being physically touched. In this documentary, the body-mind movement experience is healing. You do not need to be in the same room to experience the impact of biofield energy work. Energy transcends the confines of physical space.

If you want to find the secrets of the Universe, think in
terms of energy, frequency and vibration.

- NIKOLA TESLA

{ found joy in innovation }

When incorporating care into your wellness plan ask for trustworthy, quality referrals and vet credentials. Maintain personal boundaries, and follow your intuition. If something feels uncomfortable, stop. Christiane Northrup, M.D. states, "One of the most powerful tools for flourishing and healing is knowing how to get the right kind of support at the right time." Set an intention to find the best practitioner for you. Then, for your session, state what you want to release, and what you want to experience instead. If you are feeling stuck on one of your goals, a session could be just what's needed to release the underlying stagnant energy that is holding you back. You might also find that your mind-body-spirit has already started the self-healing process before you arrive at your session. Holistic medicine is a means to connect to that eternal, all-powerful part of you that self-heals. Sometimes results from holistic medicine modalities are seen as miraculous. I believe that miracles happen when the mind-body-spirit aligns with its true self. *Holistic medicine supports all facets of you, including self-realization.*

Miracles don't come from the cold intellect. They come from finding your authentic self and following what you feel is your own true course in life.

– BERNIE S. SIGEL, M.D.

{ finds joy in medicine }

Week No. 32 *Your Joy*

Cultivate joy! | Buy a small gift for someone just because!

Record moments of joy each day

What was your joy? Who/What gave rise to the joy? What did it feel, look, taste, smell, or sound like?

The process of reflective writing supports awareness. Awareness of what brings you joy serves as a heart-centered, resourceful compass, and unfolds more joy. The key to the journey is recognizing, understanding, and following -- your personal joy.

Joy Date · Write about your joy date - what you explored and how you felt.

Sunday _____

Monday _____

Tuesday _____

Wednesday _____

Thursday _____

Friday _____

Saturday _____

Week In Review

What was your most joyful moment this week? What themes, new or already noted, did you find in your joy moments?

The subjects have a wonderful story to tell you. And if you follow the essence -- more joy and purpose will come to light. Keep exploring your joy and add discoveries to your joy library.

Joy does not simply happen to us. We have to choose joy and keep choosing it every day.

- HENRI J.M. NOUWEN

{ found joy in spirituality }

Was any of your joy this week the product of working through fear and lessening your resistance towards a goal?

Recall scenarios where working through fear to reach a goal resulted in tremendous joy. With this awareness, in fearful moments you will find courage to move forward.

What were your achievements this week? Did you gain any new insights?

Note your most successful accomplishments, quality time with loved ones, and enlightening moments. Flip back periodically to honor your attentiveness to your priorities and review what you have learned.

Did you face challenges this week? Do you see different possibilities? How will you adjust moving forward?

Learning happens when you reflect and make adjustments to your course. Your growth is the product of working through struggles and finding a heart-centered solution. Joy resides here, too!

What kindness did you extend? How did you feel during and afterward?

Noting the kindness you extend during the week helps you to honor your light and love yourself more.

Use this space to begin planning for more joy in your life.

Dedicating time for joy makes your days brighter and more meaningful.

People

Places

Things

Experiences

Joy Date Ideas

Your Joy

Cultivate joy! | Create an at-home spa bath!

Record moments of joy each day

What was your joy? Who/What gave rise to the joy? What did it feel, look, taste, smell, or sound like?

The process of reflective writing supports awareness. Awareness of what brings you joy serves as a heart-centered, resourceful compass, and unfolds more joy. The key to the journey is recognizing, understanding, and following -- your personal joy.

Joy Date · Write about your joy date - what you explored and how you felt.

Sunday _____

Monday _____

Tuesday _____

Wednesday _____

Thursday _____

Friday _____

Saturday _____

Week In Review

What was your most joyful moment this week? What themes, new or already noted, did you find in your joy moments?

The subjects have a wonderful story to tell you. And if you follow the essence -- more joy and purpose will come to light. Keep exploring your joy and add discoveries to your joy library.

Was any of your joy this week the product of working through fear and lessening your resistance towards a goal?

Recall scenarios where working through fear to reach a goal resulted in tremendous joy. With this awareness, in fearful moments you will find courage to move forward.

What were your achievements this week? Did you gain any new insights?

Note your most successful accomplishments, quality time with loved ones, and enlightening moments. Flip back periodically to honor your attentiveness to your priorities and review what you have learned.

Did you face challenges this week? Do you see different possibilities? How will you adjust moving forward?

Learning happens when you reflect and make adjustments to your course. Your growth is the product of working through struggles and finding a heart-centered solution. Joy resides here, too!

What kindness did you extend? How did you feel during and afterward?

Noting the kindness you extend during the week helps you to honor your light and love yourself more.

Use this space to begin planning for more joy in your life.

Dedicating time for joy makes your days brighter and more meaningful.

People

Places

Things

Experiences

Joy Date Ideas

Week No. 34 *Your Joy*

Cultivate joy! | Leave a larger than normal tip!

Record moments of joy each day | What was your joy? Who/What gave rise to the joy? What did it feel, look, taste, smell, or sound like?

The process of reflective writing supports awareness. Awareness of what brings you joy serves as a heart-centered, resourceful compass, and unfolds more joy. The key to the journey is recognizing, understanding, and following -- your personal joy.

Joy Date · Write about your joy date - what you explored and how you felt.

Sunday _____

Monday _____

Tuesday _____

Wednesday _____

Thursday _____

Friday _____

Saturday _____

Week In Review

What was your most joyful moment this week? What themes, new or already noted, did you find in your joy moments?

The subjects have a wonderful story to tell you. And if you follow the essence -- more joy and purpose will come to light. Keep exploring your joy and add discoveries to your joy library.

Was any of your joy this week the product of working through fear and lessening your resistance towards a goal?

Recall scenarios where working through fear to reach a goal resulted in tremendous joy. With this awareness, in fearful moments you will find courage to move forward.

What were your achievements this week? Did you gain any new insights?

Note your most successful accomplishments, quality time with loved ones, and enlightening moments. Flip back periodically to honor your attentiveness to your priorities and review what you have learned.

Did you face challenges this week? Do you see different possibilities? How will you adjust moving forward?

Learning happens when you reflect and make adjustments to your course. Your growth is the product of working through struggles and finding a heart-centered solution. Joy resides here, too!

What kindness did you extend? How did you feel during and afterward?

Noting the kindness you extend during the week helps you to honor your light and love yourself more.

Use this space to begin planning for more joy in your life.

Dedicating time for joy makes your days brighter and more meaningful.

People

Places

Things

Experiences

Joy Date Ideas

Week No. 35 *Your Joy*

Cultivate joy! | Treat yourself to a self-care luxury that you might not otherwise!

Record moments of joy each day | What was your joy? Who/What gave rise to the joy? What did it feel, look, taste, smell, or sound like?

The process of reflective writing supports awareness. Awareness of what brings you joy serves as a heart-centered, resourceful compass, and unfolds more joy. The key to the journey is recognizing, understanding, and following -- your personal joy.

Joy Date · Write about your joy date - what you explored and how you felt.

Sunday _____

Monday _____

Tuesday _____

Wednesday _____

Thursday _____

Friday _____

Saturday _____

Week In Review

What was your most joyful moment this week? What themes, new or already noted, did you find in your joy moments?

The subjects have a wonderful story to tell you. And if you follow the essence -- more joy and purpose will come to light. Keep exploring your joy and add discoveries to your joy library.

When joy is a habit, love is a reflex.
- BOB GOEFF
{ finds joy in writing }

Was any of your joy this week the product of working through fear and lessening your resistance towards a goal?

Recall scenarios where working through fear to reach a goal resulted in tremendous joy. With this awareness, in fearful moments you will find courage to move forward.

What were your achievements this week? Did you gain any new insights?

Note your most successful accomplishments, quality time with loved ones, and enlightening moments. Flip back periodically to honor your attentiveness to your priorities and review what you have learned.

Did you face challenges this week? Do you see different possibilities? How will you adjust moving forward?

Learning happens when you reflect and make adjustments to your course. Your growth is the product of working through struggles and finding a heart-centered solution. Joy resides here, too!

What kindness did you extend? How did you feel during and afterward?

Noting the kindness you extend during the week helps you to honor your light and love yourself more.

Use this space to begin planning for more joy in your life.

Dedicating time for joy makes your days brighter and more meaningful.

People

Places

Things

Experiences

Joy Date Ideas

Your Intentions

YOUR KEYWORD

Along with your keyword, draw on the inner strength of curiosity, hope, and self-compassion as you approach your intentions.

Track the energy that you put towards your aspirations, and observe what is gained. Remember that being intentional about how you spend your time will help you achieve your goals. Where your attention goes, your energy flows.

No. 01

DESIRED GOAL:

ALCHEMY:

1	2	3	4	5	6	7
8	9	10	11	12	13	14
15	16	17	18	19	20	21
22	23	24	25	26	27	28
29	30	31				

No. 02

DESIRED GOAL:

ALCHEMY:

1	2	3	4	5	6	7
8	9	10	11	12	13	14
15	16	17	18	19	20	21
22	23	24	25	26	27	28
29	30	31				

No. 03

DESIRED GOAL:

ALCHEMY:

1	2	3	4	5	6	7
8	9	10	11	12	13	14
15	16	17	18	19	20	21
22	23	24	25	26	27	28
29	30	31				

No. 04

DESIRED GOAL:

ALCHEMY:

1	2	3	4	5	6	7
8	9	10	11	12	13	14
15	16	17	18	19	20	21
22	23	24	25	26	27	28
29	30	31				

Month In Review

Reflect on your time spent working towards your intentions.
Did you spend time as planned on your goals? Have you released what you needed to, and started to refine your focus? Record below a yes, partial, or no.

GOAL/ALCHEMY No. 01

GOAL/ALCHEMY No. 02

GOAL/ALCHEMY No. 03

GOAL/ALCHEMY No. 04

Follow effective action with quiet reflection. From the quiet reflection will come even more effective action.

- PETER F. DRUCKER

{ found joy in management }

The yesses: Congratulations! Write about your successes.
How do you feel? What does this accomplishment offer you? If you no longer need to track this goal, consider introducing a new intention from your Month No. 1 exercise.

The partials: Is there anything new that you could implement that would help you achieve your goals?
Do you need to be more intentional in setting aside time for your desires? Do you need to break the goal down into smaller steps? Be kind to yourself as you process.

The Nos: What do you think prevented you? (Be as specific and honest as possible.)
Were there influences outside of your control? Were you resistant/how? Do you want to focus on this goal next month, or start a new one? All responses provide opportunities for growth.

Head to next month's intentions journal page (p.220) and write the goals and alchemy you will focus on for the next 30 days.

Month No. 8 — Your Free Space

Create space for your dreams to materialize. As you journey, journal here about feelings, ideas, and next steps.

"I" Statements

Write positive and empowering messages.

Love

Eternity

💧 Water Rest Area

⛾ Picnic Rest Area

🥾 Vista Rest Area

Month No. 9

Raising Your Vibration with Essential Oils

Herbalism is a religion of nature, representing a balance of head and heart.

- MICHAEL TIERRA, O.M.D.

{ finds joy in herbalism }

You are a devoted adventurer getting closer to the luminous summit. I invite you to return to a quiet place and take a few deep, centering breaths. Begin to scan your body. Start at your head, and as you continue concentrating on your breath, slowly move your awareness through your whole body, working your way to your feet. Do you sense pain or tension anywhere? To gain a sense of ease, adjust your body to a more agreeable posture, lightly press on the tense space, and breathe into that area to release discomfort.

With your newfound sense of openness, imagine you are back on the enchanting forest's spiral path. As you round the bend toward Lantern No. 9, you see a beautiful cascade of light. The bright sunshine is reflecting off a group of little glass bottles placed on top of a wooden stand. The thoughtful forest wants you to take some of its energy home so that you can return to this delightful setting by smelling what it has curated for you. You pick up the bottles and notice that each carefully packaged container includes extracts of seeds, roots, bark, stems, leaves, and flowers. You open the bottles and inhale the healing aromas. You become aware that each scent creates a different feeling within you. Return to that place in your body that was tense. Do you sense more freedom in your body, mind, or spirit?

To instill a feeling of lightness and inner warmth, the intention for the ninth month is to find an essential oil, or blend, that sparks a sense of heart-healing freedom and joy within you. If you already have a favorite essential oil, I propose that you treat yourself to an additional high-vibration bottle to bring new, supportive energy into your life.

Anahata is the Sanskrit name for the fourth wheel of energy that resides at the heart center. It is the energy of transformation and is believed to be the bridge between the lower physical body and the higher spiritual, etheric bodies. When this energy center, or chakra, is open, it is a very bright green color. This month you will connect to your heart center to support your whole healing. "I am grateful" is an "I" statement.

Aromatherapy is a caring, hands-on therapy which seeks to induce relaxation, to increase energy, to reduce the effects of stress and to restore lost balance to mind, body and soul.

— ROBERT TISSERAND

{ finds joy in aromatherapy }

WHAT ARE ESSENTIAL OILS AND HOW DO YOU BENEFIT FROM THEM?

Using essential oils as a holistic healing treatment is also known as aromatherapy. This complementary therapy, originating in the ancient cultures of China, India, Israel, and Egypt, has been around for thousands of years. Essential oils are concentrated extracts of nature. The powerful healing compounds are made by steaming or cold pressing a part of a plant to extract the essence. Each essence, or element, has reported therapeutic properties that heal on physical, emotional, mental, and spiritual levels. The oils address a spectrum of health concerns, including relief from anxiety, stress, insomnia, fatigue, nausea, physical pain, skin diseases, and hormonal issues. Essential oils can support pain management, digestion, mental clarity, and promote feelings of love, relaxation, and wholeness.

TWO EFFECTIVE WAYS TO BENEFIT FROM OILS

Inhalation

Inhalation of essential oils influences the limbic system, the part of the brain that controls emotions. You can inhale directly from the bottle or place a few drops in the palm of your hand, rub your hands together, and inhale as you cup your hands around your nose and mouth. Another way to benefit from essential oils through inhalation is to use a diffuser. A diffuser breaks the oil down into smaller molecules and disperses the particles into the air before they reach your body. Additionally, you can diffuse essential oils by placing several drops into a spray bottle filled with distilled water or a 50/50 ratio of distilled water and witch hazel. Both distilled water and witch hazel help prevent bacterial growth in the bottle.

Topical

You can also benefit from essential oils by applying them topically to your skin. The skin, your largest organ, absorbs the oils, which then make their way into your bloodstream. You should dilute most oils with a carrier oil before application. The most popular carrier oils include fractionated coconut oil, olive oil, and jojoba oil. Some effective locations for physical application include your temples, heart center, the inside of your wrists, and the soles of your feet. If your skin is sensitive, the feet can be a great choice. The feet are the least sensitive skin of the entire body, and have the largest pores, so the oil is most readily absorbed. Studies show that essential oils reach the body's cells within minutes when applied to the feet. If applying to the feet, you can incorporate acupressure to strengthen the healing response. Acupressure is a way of circulating life force energy through your body's natural pathways. You can find acupressure foot maps in both aromatherapy books mentioned in the Additional References (page 295). A point of caution: You might find that your feet are slippery when you apply the oil to your soles. For safety reasons, put on socks or shoes after application.

SAFETY AND SUPPORT

Be sure that the essential oils you use are made of pure oil. Many companies create synthetic oils that can cause harm. If you are uncertain about selecting an oil you can seek help from an aromatherapist who will help guide you. If you are pregnant, nursing, taking medication, or have a medical condition, consult your healthcare provider before use.

EXPLORE BY SCENT

Here are several essential oil suggestions to explore by scent. These bright and robust oils can encourage the feelings of freedom and joy.

Citrus

Bergamot
Orange
Lemon
Grapefruit
Tangerine

Floral

Ylang Ylang
Jasmine
Rose
Palmarosa
Lavender

Woodsy

Frankincense
Idaho Blue Spruce
Copaiba
Palo Santo

Warm and Spicy

Clove
Cinnamon
Ginger
Myrrh

Musky-Earthy

Patchouli
Vetiver

Cool and Refreshing

Peppermint

Sweet

Roman Chamomile

Herbaceous

Geranium
Sage

What I Find Healing About Essential Oils

Taking a deep breath of an essential oil relaxes my body, clears my mind, lifts my spirit, and focuses my thoughts towards my desires. The action places me in my heart space of the present moment. I find that essential oils are a great tool to keep on hand to raise my vibration. I select a blend that resonates with the energy I want to feel. Oils work hand-in-hand with setting intentions because each oil has a purpose; you can find an oil that will complement your aim.

Essential oils can instill heart-centered feelings of comfort, strength, and hope. Healing your heart is integral for connecting to your true self.

There is oil in the house of the wise.

- PROVERBS 21:20

Week No. 36 Your Joy

Cultivate joy! | Leave an inspiring letter in a library book sharing what you learned!

Record moments of joy each day | What was your joy? Who/What gave rise to the joy? What did it feel, look, taste, smell, or sound like?

The process of reflective writing supports awareness. Awareness of what brings you joy serves as a heart-centered, resourceful compass, and unfolds more joy. The key to the journey is recognizing, understanding, and following -- your personal joy.

Joy Date · Write about your joy date - what you explored and how you felt.

_____

Sunday _____

Monday _____

Tuesday _____

Wednesday _____

Thursday _____

Friday _____

Saturday _____

Week In Review

What was your most joyful moment this week? What themes, new or already noted, did you find in your joy moments?

The subjects have a wonderful story to tell you. And if you follow the essence -- more joy and purpose will come to light. Keep exploring your joy and add discoveries to your joy library.

Was any of your joy this week the product of working through fear and lessening your resistance towards a goal?

Recall scenarios where working through fear to reach a goal resulted in tremendous joy. With this awareness, in fearful moments you will find courage to move forward.

What were your achievements this week? Did you gain any new insights?

Note your most successful accomplishments, quality time with loved ones, and enlightening moments. Flip back periodically to honor your attentiveness to your priorities and review what you have learned.

Did you face challenges this week? Do you see different possibilities? How will you adjust moving forward?

Learning happens when you reflect and make adjustments to your course. Your growth is the product of working through struggles and finding a heart-centered solution. Joy resides here, too!

What kindness did you extend? How did you feel during and afterward?

Noting the kindness you extend during the week helps you to honor your light and love yourself more.

Use this space to begin planning for more joy in your life.

Dedicating time for joy makes your days brighter and more meaningful.

People

Places

Things

Experiences

Joy Date Ideas

Week No. 37 *Your Joy*

Cultivate joy! | Go on a dinner date with yourself!

Record moments of joy each day

What was your joy? Who/What gave rise to the joy? What did it feel, look, taste, smell, or sound like?

The process of reflective writing supports awareness. Awareness of what brings you joy serves as a heart-centered, resourceful compass, and unfolds more joy. The key to the journey is recognizing, understanding, and following -- your personal joy.

Joy Date · Write about your joy date - what you explored and how you felt.

Sunday _____

Monday _____

Tuesday _____

Wednesday _____

Thursday _____

Friday _____

Saturday _____

Week In Review

What was your most joyful moment this week? What themes, new or already noted, did you find in your joy moments?

The subjects have a wonderful story to tell you. And if you follow the essence -- more joy and purpose will come to light. Keep exploring your joy and add discoveries to your joy library.

If you change the way you look at things, the things you look at change.

- WAYNE DYER

{ found joy in personal empowerment }

Was any of your joy this week the product of working through fear and lessening your resistance towards a goal?

Recall scenarios where working through fear to reach a goal resulted in tremendous joy. With this awareness, in fearful moments you will find courage to move forward.

What were your achievements this week? Did you gain any new insights?

Note your most successful accomplishments, quality time with loved ones, and enlightening moments. Flip back periodically to honor your attentiveness to your priorities and review what you have learned.

Did you face challenges this week? Do you see different possibilities? How will you adjust moving forward?

Learning happens when you reflect and make adjustments to your course. Your growth is the product of working through struggles and finding a heart-centered solution. Joy resides here, too!

What kindness did you extend? How did you feel during and afterward?

Noting the kindness you extend during the week helps you to honor your light and love yourself more.

Use this space to begin planning for more joy in your life.

Dedicating time for joy makes your days brighter and more meaningful.

People

Places

Things

Experiences

Joy Date Ideas

Week No. 38 *Your Joy*

Cultivate joy! | Send someone a book that you think they will enjoy!

Record moments of joy each day | What was your joy? Who/What gave rise to the joy? What did it feel, look, taste, smell, or sound like?

The process of reflective writing supports awareness. Awareness of what brings you joy serves as a heart-centered, resourceful compass, and unfolds more joy. The key to the journey is recognizing, understanding, and following -- your personal joy.

Joy Date · Write about your joy date - what you explored and how you felt.

Sunday _____

Monday _____

Tuesday _____

Wednesday _____

Thursday _____

Friday _____

Saturday _____

Week In Review

What was your most joyful moment this week? What themes, new or already noted, did you find in your joy moments?

The subjects have a wonderful story to tell you. And if you follow the essence -- more joy and purpose will come to light. Keep exploring your joy and add discoveries to your joy library.

Was any of your joy this week the product of working through fear and lessening your resistance towards a goal?

Recall scenarios where working through fear to reach a goal resulted in tremendous joy. With this awareness, in fearful moments you will find courage to move forward.

What were your achievements this week? Did you gain any new insights?

Note your most successful accomplishments, quality time with loved ones, and enlightening moments. Flip back periodically to honor your attentiveness to your priorities and review what you have learned.

Did you face challenges this week? Do you see different possibilities? How will you adjust moving forward?

Learning happens when you reflect and make adjustments to your course. Your growth is the product of working through struggles and finding a heart-centered solution. Joy resides here, too!

What kindness did you extend? How did you feel during and afterward?

Noting the kindness you extend during the week helps you to honor your light and love yourself more.

Use this space to begin planning for more joy in your life.

Dedicating time for joy makes your days brighter and more meaningful.

People

Places

Things

Experiences

Joy Date Ideas

Week No. 39  *Your Joy*

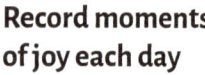

Cultivate joy! | Take a rest from social media!

Record moments of joy each day | What was your joy? Who/What gave rise to the joy? What did it feel, look, taste, smell, or sound like?

The process of reflective writing supports awareness. Awareness of what brings you joy serves as a heart-centered, resourceful compass, and unfolds more joy. The key to the journey is recognizing, understanding, and following -- your personal joy.

Joy Date · Write about your joy date - what you explored and how you felt.

Sunday _____

Monday _____

Tuesday _____

Wednesday _____

Thursday _____

Friday _____

Saturday _____

Week In Review

What was your most joyful moment this week? What themes, new or already noted, did you find in your joy moments?

The subjects have a wonderful story to tell you. And if you follow the essence -- more joy and purpose will come to light. Keep exploring your joy and add discoveries to your joy library.

Was any of your joy this week the product of working through fear and lessening your resistance towards a goal?

Recall scenarios where working through fear to reach a goal resulted in tremendous joy. With this awareness, in fearful moments you will find courage to move forward.

What were your achievements this week? Did you gain any new insights?

Note your most successful accomplishments, quality time with loved ones, and enlightening moments. Flip back periodically to honor your attentiveness to your priorities and review what you have learned.

Did you face challenges this week? Do you see different possibilities? How will you adjust moving forward?

Learning happens when you reflect and make adjustments to your course. Your growth is the product of working through struggles and finding a heart-centered solution. Joy resides here, too!

What kindness did you extend? How did you feel during and afterward?

Noting the kindness you extend during the week helps you to honor your light and love yourself more.

Use this space to begin planning for more joy in your life.

Dedicating time for joy makes your days brighter and more meaningful.

People

Places

Things

Experiences

Joy Date Ideas

Your Intentions

YOUR KEYWORD

Along with your keyword, draw on the inner strength of curiosity, hope, and self-compassion as you approach your intentions.

Track the energy that you put towards your aspirations, and observe what is gained. Remember that being intentional about how you spend your time will help you achieve your goals. Where your attention goes, your energy flows.

No. 01

DESIRED GOAL:

ALCHEMY:

1	2	3	4	5	6	7
8	9	10	11	12	13	14
15	16	17	18	19	20	21
22	23	24	25	26	27	28
29	30	31				

No. 02

DESIRED GOAL:

ALCHEMY:

1	2	3	4	5	6	7
8	9	10	11	12	13	14
15	16	17	18	19	20	21
22	23	24	25	26	27	28
29	30	31				

No. 03

DESIRED GOAL:

ALCHEMY:

1	2	3	4	5	6	7
8	9	10	11	12	13	14
15	16	17	18	19	20	21
22	23	24	25	26	27	28
29	30	31				

No. 04

DESIRED GOAL:

ALCHEMY:

1	2	3	4	5	6	7
8	9	10	11	12	13	14
15	16	17	18	19	20	21
22	23	24	25	26	27	28
29	30	31				

Month In Review

Reflect on your time spent working towards your intentions.

Did you spend time as planned on your goals? Have you released what you needed to, and started to refine your focus? Record below a yes, partial, or no.

GOAL/ALCHEMY No. 01

GOAL/ALCHEMY No. 02

GOAL/ALCHEMY No. 03

GOAL/ALCHEMY No. 04

The best way to predict the future is to invent it.

- ALAN KAY

{ finds joy in innovation }

The yesses: Congratulations! Write about your successes.

How do you feel? What does this accomplishment offer you? If you no longer need to track this goal, consider introducing a new intention from your Month No. 1 exercise.

The partials: Is there anything new that you could implement that would help you achieve your goals?

Do you need to be more intentional in setting aside time for your desires? Do you need to break the goal down into smaller steps? Be kind to yourself as you process.

The Nos: What do you think prevented you? (Be as specific and honest as possible.)

Were there influences outside of your control? Were you resistant/how? Do you want to focus on this goal next month, or start a new one? All responses provide opportunities for growth.

Head to next month's intentions journal page (p.242) and write the goals and alchemy you will focus on for the next 30 days.

Month No. 9 Your Free Space

Create space for your dreams to materialize. As you journey, journal here about feelings, ideas, and next steps.

"I" Statements

Write positive and empowering messages.

Vista Rest Area

Feeling exceptionally light and giddy from the gifts at lantern No. 9, you are floating on the path at this point of the adventure. You begin to wonder if you are delirious. Up ahead, you see the path change form. Here, the natural path transforms into metal. As if you are at the airport, you step onto a slowly moving walkway. At first level to the ground, over time, the walkway ascends. The climb feels as if you are rising in a skyscraper. Your ears pop, your inner bearings shift, and like all great elevators, there is lift music, "I am...I Said" by Neil Diamond is piping through the air. You are gliding higher, thinking about your aspirations, and who you are. At the very top of the ride, the music fades. The silence, the crisp fresh air, and the vista are awe-inspiring. You sense you have reached a peak of the tallest mountain. You rest here and take in the elevated perspective for as long as you like.

Often on a rigorous hike, you spend a lot of time looking at the ground ahead of you. This rest stop is a reminder to look up and to take in the wider viewpoint.

A Precious Human Life

Every day, think as you wake up

Today I am fortunate to have woken up.

I am alive, I have a precious human life.

I am not going to waste it. I am going to use all my energies

to develop myself, expand my heart out to others,

to achieve enlightenment for the benefit of all beings.

I am going to have kind thoughts towards others.

I am not going to get angry, or think badly about others.

I am going to benefit others as much as I can.

- HIS HOLINESS THE XIVTH THE DALAI LAMA

{ finds joy in compassion }

Love

Eternity

🜄 Water Rest Area

⊼ Picnic Rest Area

↗ Vista Rest Area

Month No. 10

Communing with an Altar

Listen to the wind, it talks. Listen to the silence, it speaks.
Listen to your heart, it knows.

- NATIVE AMERICAN PROVERB

This page marks your arrival at mile-marker No. 10 on the flourishing path. You are three-quarters of the way en route to your destination. You have reached another inward-turning point. Before proceeding, take time to pay tribute to the joy that you have experienced, all you have worked through and towards, and the gifts the enchanted forest has lovingly offered to you.

As a way to honor your journey, you decide to rest a bit longer by the light of lantern No. 10. You unroll your meditation mat, sit down, and begin to reflect on all that you have collected. You have your joy journaling pages, your intention awareness pages, your vision, your golden feather pen, your magical magnifying glass, sage, palo santo, a mirror with magic powers, your meditation rug, prayer beads, your journal, and your essential oils. You pull your tools from your travel bag and place them in front of you. You think how nice it would be, once you get home, to thoughtfully put them somewhere special so that you can utilize these meaningful items and continue your transformation. Close your eyes and imagine the perfect place in your home to keep them gathered. What did you see?

The intention for the tenth month is to create a home altar. A home altar is a sacred place to house your prayers, symbols of your love, and healing tools. It is a structure for ritual, strength, and guidance. If you already have a home altar, this month, I propose cleaning and refreshing your altar to bring in more loving energy.

Indigo is the color of the sixth chakra, Anja. This energy center represents your celestial body. Its focus is your higher feeling and includes your intuition, imagination, and the statement, "I see." This month you will connect to your clear seeing to manifest your desires.

CREATING YOUR HOME ALTAR

Start by identifying an area for your altar. This space does not need to be grand; it can be as small as a corner of your nightstand. The location that came to mind in the meditation could be an excellent option. Once you have cleared a space, consider the construction of the altar. A joy date can be a wonderful opportunity to search for your altar. You can make an altar out of anything that feels right for you. My altar is a small narrow wooden table, and the tabletop is hand-carved with a scene from India. I purchased this table at a second-hand store. The moment I spotted it, I knew it would make a perfect altar. On your altar, place meaningful items that represent your prayers and objects that instill a feeling of peace and devotion. What you gather on and around the space of an altar is a form of communication with God/the Universe. These objects could include photographs, prayer cards, meaningful jewelry, inspirational quotes, books, or intentions written on paper. A large Rose Quartz heart resides in the center of my altar. On my altar, I keep a pin that reads, "I believe in magic." I also keep a Mother's Day card from my children with the words, "Best Mom Ever." Three Guatemalan worry dolls rest in their box on my altar. They represent my children and me, their presence is a steady request to God/the Universe to nurture us and to help resolve our fears. A tiny Buddha, gifted by a dear friend, sits on my altar watching over my wishes and reminds me of the gift of friendship. A silver angel ornament, given to me by someone who warmly supported the sales arm of my clothing company, is another treasured item displayed on my altar. It is engraved with the words, "From small beginnings come great things."

3 MAIN ALTAR ELEMENTS

1. Locate a space for your altar: a small table, your nightstand, a window ledge, a corner of your deck, or a place in your garden.

2. Place meaningful items on your altar: gifts, photographs, inspirational quotes, books, your intentions, and prayers. Include natural elements, such as crystals, stones, flowers, and treasures from your travels and life experiences.

3. Create a ritual to honor your altar: Burn incense and light candles, meditate, practice yoga and your form of prayer.

 You may find it beneficial to periodically cleanse and recharge your gemstones, at times placed on your altar. This can be done several ways. Place them in moonlight, sunlight, salt, smudge with sage, or create a combination of any of the above. Do what feels best for you!

When we say a prayer, we allow our consciousness to receive intuitive guidance.

- GABBY BERNSTEIN

{ finds joy in spirituality }

How I Find Support in an Altar

I feel support within the essence of my altar. It's one of my most meaningful ways of communicating with God/the Universe. When I place something on or around my altar, it signals that it is important to me. I am announcing a desire, and am open to how it unfolds. The items I place upon this sacred pillar are my most heartfelt wishes. My offerings allow me to feel reassured that my heart and my manifestations are heard and materializing. They also reiterate that I trust in the process, and understand there is a bigger picture. I can appreciate the silent movement of God/the Universe. Sometimes I would prefer to make swift decisions and tidy up. I have learned to be patient, allow space, and sense in my heart when an element still needs nurturing, and when it is resolved and ready for forward momentum. The process helps me cultivate a centered stillness, appreciation for listening inward, and clarity.

Mathematics is the language with which
God has written the Universe.

- GALILEO GALILEI

{ found joy in the stars }

A PENDULUM

Another tool that has helped hone my intuition is a pendulum. Sometimes my pendulum rests on my altar. A pendulum is a weight suspended from a pivot. Pendulums have been a scientific form of measurement for centuries. The pendulum has many applications. It measures time - the pendulum clock design superseded the quartz clock design. The pendulum measures acceleration - earthquake and volcanic movement, and gravity. [20] The pendulum measures your intuition, too. To use a pendulum to gauge your inner compass, first, hold your pendulum at a pivot point. Then, to assure you are working from your higher self, request, or intend that your ego self step aside. Once you feel centered in your true self, ask the pendulum to swing in a direction to indicate a yes. You most likely will see the weight start swinging. Then, ask your pendulum to indicate the direction of a no. Most likely, the weight will swing in an alternate direction. Attuning to your pendulum can take practice, be patient and practice often. Once you feel comfortable, you can apply this query process to situations in which you need support. In time, you will find that you rely less on your pendulum and can simply sense a stronger and more clear internal indication.

Sense the love and joy that manifest as you connect deeper to yourself.
Become aware of the support, clarity, and calm you gain.

The spiritual path is a rigorous journey, one that takes the rest of your life. The goal is the liberation of your spirit – of your capacity to love without fear and receive love and rise to your fullest creative potential.

– CAROLINE MYSS

{ finds joy in the mystic }

Week No. 40 *Your Joy*

Cultivate joy! | Send dessert to another table!

Record moments of joy each day

What was your joy? Who/What gave rise to the joy?
What did it feel, look, taste, smell, or sound like?

The process of reflective writing supports awareness. Awareness of what brings you joy serves as a heart-centered, resourceful compass, and unfolds more joy. The key to the journey is recognizing, understanding, and following -- your personal joy.

Joy Date · Write about your joy date - what you explored and how you felt.

Sunday _____

Monday _____

Tuesday _____

Wednesday _____

Thursday _____

Friday _____

Saturday _____

Week In Review

What was your most joyful moment this week? What themes, new or already noted, did you find in your joy moments?

The subjects have a wonderful story to tell you. And if you follow the essence -- more joy and purpose will come to light. Keep exploring your joy and add discoveries to your joy library.

Was any of your joy this week the product of working through fear and lessening your resistance towards a goal?

Recall scenarios where working through fear to reach a goal resulted in tremendous joy. With this awareness, in fearful moments you will find courage to move forward.

What were your achievements this week? Did you gain any new insights?

Note your most successful accomplishments, quality time with loved ones, and enlightening moments. Flip back periodically to honor your attentiveness to your priorities and review what you have learned.

Did you face challenges this week? Do you see different possibilities? How will you adjust moving forward?

Learning happens when you reflect and make adjustments to your course. Your growth is the product of working through struggles and finding a heart-centered solution. Joy resides here, too!

What kindness did you extend? How did you feel during and afterward?

Noting the kindness you extend during the week helps you to honor your light and love yourself more.

Use this space to begin planning for more joy in your life.

Dedicating time for joy makes your days brighter and more meaningful.

People

Places

Things

Experiences

Joy Date Ideas

Week No. 41

Your Joy

Cultivate joy! | Can't travel? Create a virtual vacation with family and/or friends!

Record moments of joy each day | What was your joy? Who/What gave rise to the joy? What did it feel, look, taste, smell, or sound like?

The process of reflective writing supports awareness. Awareness of what brings you joy serves as a heart-centered, resourceful compass, and unfolds more joy. The key to the journey is recognizing, understanding, and following -- your personal joy.

Joy Date · Write about your joy date - what you explored and how you felt.

Sunday _____

Monday _____

Tuesday _____

Wednesday _____

Thursday _____

Friday _____

Saturday _____

Week In Review

What was your most joyful moment this week? What themes, new or already noted, did you find in your joy moments?

The subjects have a wonderful story to tell you. And if you follow the essence -- more joy and purpose will come to light. Keep exploring your joy and add discoveries to your joy library.

Was any of your joy this week the product of working through fear and lessening your resistance towards a goal?

Recall scenarios where working through fear to reach a goal resulted in tremendous joy. With this awareness, in fearful moments you will find courage to move forward.

What were your achievements this week? Did you gain any new insights?

Note your most successful accomplishments, quality time with loved ones, and enlightening moments. Flip back periodically to honor your attentiveness to your priorities and review what you have learned.

Did you face challenges this week? Do you see different possibilities? How will you adjust moving forward?

Learning happens when you reflect and make adjustments to your course. Your growth is the product of working through struggles and finding a heart-centered solution. Joy resides here, too!

What kindness did you extend? How did you feel during and afterward?

Noting the kindness you extend during the week helps you to honor your light and love yourself more.

Use this space to begin planning for more joy in your life.

Dedicating time for joy makes your days brighter and more meaningful.

People

Places

Things

Experiences

Joy Date Ideas

Week No. 42 *Your Joy*

Cultivate joy! | Handwrite a thank you note next time you are about to text "thank you!"

Record moments of joy each day | What was your joy? Who/What gave rise to the joy? What did it feel, look, taste, smell, or sound like?

The process of reflective writing supports awareness. Awareness of what brings you joy serves as a heart-centered, resourceful compass, and unfolds more joy. The key to the journey is recognizing, understanding, and following -- your personal joy.

Joy Date · Write about your joy date - what you explored and how you felt.

Sunday _____

Monday _____

Tuesday _____

Wednesday _____

Thursday _____

Friday _____

Saturday _____

Week In Review

What was your most joyful moment this week? What themes, new or already noted, did you find in your joy moments?

The subjects have a wonderful story to tell you. And if you follow the essence -- more joy and purpose will come to light. Keep exploring your joy and add discoveries to your joy library.

Was any of your joy this week the product of working through fear and lessening your resistance towards a goal?

Recall scenarios where working through fear to reach a goal resulted in tremendous joy. With this awareness, in fearful moments you will find courage to move forward.

What were your achievements this week? Did you gain any new insights?

Note your most successful accomplishments, quality time with loved ones, and enlightening moments. Flip back periodically to honor your attentiveness to your priorities and review what you have learned.

Did you face challenges this week? Do you see different possibilities? How will you adjust moving forward?

Learning happens when you reflect and make adjustments to your course. Your growth is the product of working through struggles and finding a heart-centered solution. Joy resides here, too!

What kindness did you extend? How did you feel during and afterward?

Noting the kindness you extend during the week helps you to honor your light and love yourself more.

Use this space to begin planning for more joy in your life.

Dedicating time for joy makes your days brighter and more meaningful.

People

Places

Things

Experiences

Joy Date Ideas

Week No. 43 *Your Joy*

Cultivate joy! | Simplify your to-do list!

Record moments of joy each day | What was your joy? Who/What gave rise to the joy? What did it feel, look, taste, smell, or sound like?

The process of reflective writing supports awareness. Awareness of what brings you joy serves as a heart-centered, resourceful compass, and unfolds more joy. The key to the journey is recognizing, understanding, and following -- your personal joy.

Joy Date · Write about your joy date - what you explored and how you felt.

Sunday _____

Monday _____

Tuesday _____

Wednesday _____

Thursday _____

Friday _____

Saturday _____

Week In Review

What was your most joyful moment this week? What themes, new or already noted, did you find in your joy moments?

The subjects have a wonderful story to tell you. And if you follow the essence -- more joy and purpose will come to light. Keep exploring your joy and add discoveries to your joy library.

Find a place inside where there's joy, and the joy will burn out the pain.

- JOSEPH CAMPBELL

{ found joy in studying the human experience }

Was any of your joy this week the product of working through fear and lessening your resistance towards a goal?

Recall scenarios where working through fear to reach a goal resulted in tremendous joy. With this awareness, in fearful moments you will find courage to move forward.

What were your achievements this week? Did you gain any new insights?

Note your most successful accomplishments, quality time with loved ones, and enlightening moments. Flip back periodically to honor your attentiveness to your priorities and review what you have learned.

Did you face challenges this week? Do you see different possibilities? How will you adjust moving forward?

Learning happens when you reflect and make adjustments to your course. Your growth is the product of working through struggles and finding a heart-centered solution. Joy resides here, too!

What kindness did you extend? How did you feel during and afterward?

Noting the kindness you extend during the week helps you to honor your light and love yourself more.

Use this space to begin planning for more joy in your life.

Dedicating time for joy makes your days brighter and more meaningful.

People

Places

Things

Experiences

Joy Date Ideas

Week No. 44 *Your Joy*

Cultivate joy! | Buy two bright candles, gift one!

Record moments of joy each day

What was your joy? Who/What gave rise to the joy? What did it feel, look, taste, smell, or sound like?

The process of reflective writing supports awareness. Awareness of what brings you joy serves as a heart-centered, resourceful compass, and unfolds more joy. The key to the journey is recognizing, understanding, and following -- your personal joy.

Joy Date · Write about your joy date - what you explored and how you felt.

Sunday _____

Monday _____

Tuesday _____

Wednesday _____

Thursday _____

Friday _____

Saturday _____

Week In Review

What was your most joyful moment this week? What themes, new or already noted, did you find in your joy moments?

The subjects have a wonderful story to tell you. And if you follow the essence -- more joy and purpose will come to light. Keep exploring your joy and add discoveries to your joy library.

Success is liking yourself, liking what you do, and liking how you do it.

- MAYA ANGELOU

{ found joy in advocating }

Was any of your joy this week the product of working through fear and lessening your resistance towards a goal?

Recall scenarios where working through fear to reach a goal resulted in tremendous joy. With this awareness, in fearful moments you will find courage to move forward.

What were your achievements this week? Did you gain any new insights?

Note your most successful accomplishments, quality time with loved ones, and enlightening moments. Flip back periodically to honor your attentiveness to your priorities and review what you have learned.

Did you face challenges this week? Do you see different possibilities? How will you adjust moving forward?

Learning happens when you reflect and make adjustments to your course. Your growth is the product of working through struggles and finding a heart-centered solution. Joy resides here, too!

What kindness did you extend? How did you feel during and afterward?

Noting the kindness you extend during the week helps you to honor your light and love yourself more.

Use this space to begin planning for more joy in your life.

Dedicating time for joy makes your days brighter and more meaningful.

People

Places

Things

Experiences

Joy Date Ideas

Month No. 10 *Your Intentions*

YOUR KEYWORD

Along with your keyword, draw on the inner strength of curiosity, hope, and self-compassion as you approach your intentions.

Track the energy that you put towards your aspirations, and observe what is gained. Remember that being intentional about how you spend your time will help you achieve your goals. Where your attention goes, your energy flows.

No. 01
DESIRED GOAL:

ALCHEMY:

1	2	3	4	5	6	7
8	9	10	11	12	13	14
15	16	17	18	19	20	21
22	23	24	25	26	27	28
29	30	31				

No. 02
DESIRED GOAL:

ALCHEMY:

1	2	3	4	5	6	7
8	9	10	11	12	13	14
15	16	17	18	19	20	21
22	23	24	25	26	27	28
29	30	31				

No. 03
DESIRED GOAL:

ALCHEMY:

1	2	3	4	5	6	7
8	9	10	11	12	13	14
15	16	17	18	19	20	21
22	23	24	25	26	27	28
29	30	31				

No. 04
DESIRED GOAL:

ALCHEMY:

1	2	3	4	5	6	7
8	9	10	11	12	13	14
15	16	17	18	19	20	21
22	23	24	25	26	27	28
29	30	31				

Month In Review

Reflect on your time spent working towards your intentions.

Did you spend time as planned on your goals? Have you released what you needed to, and started to refine your focus? Record below a yes, partial, or no.

GOAL/ALCHEMY No. 01

GOAL/ALCHEMY No. 02

GOAL/ALCHEMY No. 03

GOAL/ALCHEMY No. 04

You can be anything you want to be, do anything you set out to accomplish, if you hold to that desire and singleness of purpose.

- ABRAHAM LINCOLN

{ found joy in freedom }

The yesses: Congratulations! Write about your successes.

How do you feel? What does this accomplishment offer you? If you no longer need to track this goal, consider introducing a new intention from your Month No. 1 exercise.

The partials: Is there anything new that you could implement that would help you achieve your goals?

Do you need to be more intentional in setting aside time for your desires? Do you need to break the goal down into smaller steps? Be kind to yourself as you process.

The Nos: What do you think prevented you? (Be as specific and honest as possible.)

Were there influences outside of your control? Were you resistant/how? Do you want to focus on this goal next month, or start a new one? All responses provide opportunities for growth

Head to next month's intentions journal page (p.260) and write the goals and alchemy you will focus on for the next 30 days.

Month No. 10 *Your Free Space*

Create space for your dreams to materialize. As you journey, journal here about feelings, ideas, and next steps.

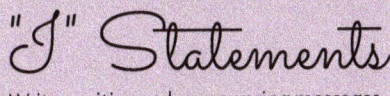

"I" Statements

Write positive and empowering messages.

Month No. 11

Feeling Safe and Grounded

If you are depressed you are living in the past, if you are anxious you are living in the future, if you are at peace, you are living in the present.

- LAO TZU

{ found joy in philosophy }

You have reached mile-marker No. 11 of the Flourish journey right on time. The final two months of the path remain on the horizon. Like most adventures, as you near the conclusion, part of you might be excited to reach the final destination, and part of you might wish the journey would continue. You feel a desire to return to the familiar, yet you also sense that you have changed and can no longer go back to what was.

As you approach the light of lantern No. 11, you see a large rattlesnake ahead of you in the middle of your path. This rattlesnake makes you feel very uneasy as he looks directly at you, and hisses. You consider retreating backward slowly for safety. As you turn your head to look behind, you see a wild boar. You are now frozen - you can't move forward or backward. You think this is cruel of the forest that has been so friendly and supportive at all the other stops. Maybe you do want to go home! You consider clicking your heels like Dorothy. Your heart is racing. You can't seem to calm yourself to think clearly and format a plan to feel secure. You look up, and at this moment, a hawk is soaring overhead and floats an envelope down to you. You reach for the letter that has your name on the cover. You begin reading the illuminated words, and they outline ways to feel centered, grounded, and serene. As you read the directions and try the ideas, you feel at peace. As this inner shift occurs, you look ahead and behind you on the path and notice that both the rattlesnake and the wild boar disappeared. With a sigh of relief, you can now see the good in this brief interlude as you have gained more helpful tools on your journey.

The aim of the eleventh month is for you to explore and find supportive grounding techniques that shift you away from scattered, overwhelmed, or fearful states into a tranquil space.

Red is the color of the Root Chakra, the energy center of security, grounding, and physical sensation. This month you will connect to the first chakra, Muladhara, to feel safe and secure. A supportive "I" statement is, "I am grounded."

ABOUT GROUNDING

Grounding is an energetic process of cleansing and balancing your energy by connecting to the stabilizing Earth's energy. Grounding techniques help shift fear-based feelings such as anxiety and anger to a centered and lighter vibration of peace and calm. Recent scientific research has explored that grounding can be potentially beneficial for physical healing too. [21] Highly Sensitive People and empaths, who tend to sense and take in other people's energy more easily, often find grounding a supportive technique because it helps keep them in their personal energy field, absorbing less from others.

Grounding is similar to the physics of electricity. Think about an electrical circuit and how a grounding wire discharges excess electrical current; grounding techniques dispel excess energy in your body. There are several approaches. Here are a few examples. Discover the best techniques for you, and incorporate what feels comfortable into your daily routine.

EARTHING

Picture your energy radiating from the soles of your feet extending to the core of the Earth. Make sure the image you have of the core feels safe and comforting. The core is made of a nickel-iron alloy and is about the same temperature as the sun. It was not until I changed my perception of the core to a supportive place that I was able to ground. The key is to find a peaceful feeling as you move your awareness from your head to your feet and then extend that energy deeper into the Earth's core. You may go further with this exercise by bringing the Earth's energy back up through your legs, then through your torso, and up through your head as if one loop of energy is circulating amongst you and the Earth. Picture this as a rubber band loop of energy, or see it as the roundabout motion of a Ferris wheel. A different image may emerge in your mind and if so, go with that instead. You will feel a magnetic connection and become calm with practice.

GEMSTONES

The Earth provides us a wide range of energies in the form of crystals and gemstones. These healing elements are created from minerals that first originate from magma. The magma surfaces from the core to the Earth's crust at a varying pace, sometimes over billions of years, and through this migration forms a unique structure. Each stone has a distinctive vibration that is created by the back and forth motion of its particles. The individual journey of formation creates the special makeup of each stone, much like our individual journeys that make each of us unique.

From an energy perspective, the human body resonates with and attunes to the higher vibrations of the stone's natural energetic properties. If you have picked up a Quartz crystal and felt a tingle or surge in your body that is most likely because the energy of the stone transformed into an electrical charge when it came into contact with your body heat. Quartz is a highly conductive and valuable stone, used to make clocks, phones, computers, and navigational equipment. The healing effects of gemstones are usually subtle. Keep working with them, and over time you likely will feel the energy they have to provide. Even if you don't feel something, know the energy is supporting you.

There are a variety of grounding gemstones. My favorites include Black Onyx, Smokey Quartz, Green Moss Agate, Petrified Wood, and Red Jasper. Carry a piece of gemstone - or your prayer beads - on your body, in your pocket, or in your purse. If you are not holding the stones, connect to the energy of the stone with your imagination. The connection is achieved by becoming aware of your point of consciousness and then shifting it to the location of your stone to feel grounded. The idea of connecting to something outside of your physical touch is similar to reflecting upon your joy. The composer Richard Rodgers expressed this notion well in the lyrics of "My Favorite Things", "I simply remember some of my favorite things, and then I don't feel so bad."

NATURE

If possible, garden or spend time walking in nature, barefoot. Making contact with the ground connects your energy to the Earth. Water is also grounding. Walking the beach, swimming, and taking a shower or bath, are all grounding activities. When showering, experiment bathing with a home-made scrub combination of 1/2 part baking soda and 1/2 part coarse sea salt, and when taking a bath, add Epsom salt - both are antidotes for removing old energy from your whole body. The ocean and natural hot springs are great for energy cleansing, too!

YOGA

If possible, create a regular yoga practice. Yoga is both grounding and heart-opening. To strengthen your grounding connection while practicing, be mindful of your connection to the Earth through the surface of your hands and the soles of your feet. I find many of my brightest thoughts and most creative ideas arrive while I'm doing yoga.

CONNECT YOUR BREATH AND HEART

When practicing grounding techniques, be sure to begin by setting the intention to ground yourself. Then pay close attention to your breath, focus on becoming one with your breath, and move your point of consciousness to your heart. Watching your breath helps you stay in the present moment, consciously connected to your body; and concentrating on your open heart keeps you heart centered. Once you are aware of your breath, add in a joyful image of a person, place, thing, or experience to make the process more elevating and, therefore, more healing. The combination of focused heart-centered breathing and "activating a positive feeling" is my short adaptation of a more lengthy *2-Step Meditation for Inner Peace and Calm with Heart-Brain Quick Coherence Technique* written by Gregg Braden. The process links your heart and brain, and over time with practice, it is believed that you can cultivate peace quickly and hold a serene feeling for a longer duration. [22]

A Grounding Event in My Life

I felt an energetic surge run through my entire body and ground me firmly to the Earth while having an unhealthy marriage conversation. The energy empowered me to work through my long-standing, overwhelming fears about going through a divorce. These fears included hurting others, namely my children and family, breaking a commitment, the unknown, and other people's opinions. I also more deeply recognized a supportive higher power at work a few months later when a medical reimbursement check synchronistically arrived in the mail from my lumpectomy surgery, sixteen months prior. The value of the unexpected check was what I needed for a new apartment security deposit due in two days time. I share these experiences to complete threads in my story and to inspire faith in yours.

Feeling peaceful and serene is your true nature.

God grant me the serenity to accept the things I cannot change; courage to change the things I can; and wisdom to know the difference.

- REINHOLD NIEBUHR

{ found joy in theology }

Week No. 45 *Your Joy*

Cultivate joy! | Be someone's cheerleader!

Record moments of joy each day

What was your joy? Who/What gave rise to the joy? What did it feel, look, taste, smell, or sound like?

The process of reflective writing supports awareness. Awareness of what brings you joy serves as a heart-centered, resourceful compass, and unfolds more joy. The key to the journey is recognizing, understanding, and following -- your personal joy.

Joy Date · Write about your joy date - what you explored and how you felt.

Sunday _____

Monday _____

Tuesday _____

Wednesday _____

Thursday _____

Friday _____

Saturday _____

Week In Review

What was your most joyful moment this week? What themes, new or already noted, did you find in your joy moments?

The subjects have a wonderful story to tell you. And if you follow the essence -- more joy and purpose will come to light. Keep exploring your joy and add discoveries to your joy library.

Was any of your joy this week the product of working through fear and lessening your resistance towards a goal?

Recall scenarios where working through fear to reach a goal resulted in tremendous joy. With this awareness, in fearful moments you will find courage to move forward.

What were your achievements this week? Did you gain any new insights?

Note your most successful accomplishments, quality time with loved ones, and enlightening moments. Flip back periodically to honor your attentiveness to your priorities and review what you have learned.

Did you face challenges this week? Do you see different possibilities? How will you adjust moving forward?

Learning happens when you reflect and make adjustments to your course. Your growth is the product of working through struggles and finding a heart-centered solution. Joy resides here, too!

What kindness did you extend? How did you feel during and afterward?

Noting the kindness you extend during the week helps you to honor your light and love yourself more.

Use this space to begin planning for more joy in your life.

Dedicating time for joy makes your days brighter and more meaningful.

People

Places

Things

Experiences

Joy Date Ideas

Week No. 46 *Your Joy*

Cultivate joy! | Be on time!

Record moments of joy each day

What was your joy? Who/What gave rise to the joy? What did it feel, look, taste, smell, or sound like?

The process of reflective writing supports awareness. Awareness of what brings you joy serves as a heart-centered, resourceful compass, and unfolds more joy. The key to the journey is recognizing, understanding, and following -- your personal joy.

Joy Date · Write about your joy date - what you explored and how you felt.

Sunday _____

Monday _____

Tuesday _____

Wednesday _____

Thursday _____

Friday _____

Saturday _____

Week In Review

What was your most joyful moment this week? What themes, new or already noted, did you find in your joy moments?

The subjects have a wonderful story to tell you. And if you follow the essence -- more joy and purpose will come to light. Keep exploring your joy and add discoveries to your joy library.

All of our dreams come true if we have the courage to pursue them.

— WALT DISNEY

{ found joy in innovation }

Was any of your joy this week the product of working through fear and lessening your resistance towards a goal?

Recall scenarios where working through fear to reach a goal resulted in tremendous joy. With this awareness, in fearful moments you will find courage to move forward.

What were your achievements this week? Did you gain any new insights?

Note your most successful accomplishments, quality time with loved ones, and enlightening moments. Flip back periodically to honor your attentiveness to your priorities and review what you have learned.

Did you face challenges this week? Do you see different possibilities? How will you adjust moving forward?

Learning happens when you reflect and make adjustments to your course. Your growth is the product of working through struggles and finding a heart-centered solution. Joy resides here, too!

What kindness did you extend? How did you feel during and afterward?

Noting the kindness you extend during the week helps you to honor your light and love yourself more.

Use this space to begin planning for more joy in your life.

Dedicating time for joy makes your days brighter and more meaningful.

People

Places

Things

Experiences

Joy Date Ideas

255

Week No. 47 *Your Joy*

Cultivate joy! | Write your future self a letter of advice!

Record moments of joy each day | What was your joy? Who/What gave rise to the joy? What did it feel, look, taste, smell, or sound like?

The process of reflective writing supports awareness. Awareness of what brings you joy serves as a heart-centered, resourceful compass, and unfolds more joy. The key to the journey is recognizing, understanding, and following -- your personal joy.

Joy Date · Write about your joy date - what you explored and how you felt.

Sunday _____

Monday _____

Tuesday _____

Wednesday _____

Thursday _____

Friday _____

Saturday _____

Week In Review

What was your most joyful moment this week? What themes, new or already noted, did you find in your joy moments?

The subjects have a wonderful story to tell you. And if you follow the essence -- more joy and purpose will come to light. Keep exploring your joy and add discoveries to your joy library.

Was any of your joy this week the product of working through fear and lessening your resistance towards a goal?

Recall scenarios where working through fear to reach a goal resulted in tremendous joy. With this awareness, in fearful moments you will find courage to move forward.

What were your achievements this week? Did you gain any new insights?

Note your most successful accomplishments, quality time with loved ones, and enlightening moments. Flip back periodically to honor your attentiveness to your priorities and review what you have learned.

Did you face challenges this week? Do you see different possibilities? How will you adjust moving forward?

Learning happens when you reflect and make adjustments to your course. Your growth is the product of working through struggles and finding a heart-centered solution. Joy resides here, too!

What kindness did you extend? How did you feel during and afterward?

Noting the kindness you extend during the week helps you to honor your light and love yourself more.

Use this space to begin planning for more joy in your life.

Dedicating time for joy makes your days brighter and more meaningful.

People

Places

Things

Experiences

Joy Date Ideas

Week No. 48 — *Your Joy*

Cultivate joy! | Compliment a stranger!

Record moments of joy each day | What was your joy? Who/What gave rise to the joy? What did it feel, look, taste, smell, or sound like?

The process of reflective writing supports awareness. Awareness of what brings you joy serves as a heart-centered, resourceful compass, and unfolds more joy. The key to the journey is recognizing, understanding, and following -- your personal joy.

Joy Date · Write about your joy date - what you explored and how you felt.

Sunday _____

Monday _____

Tuesday _____

Wednesday _____

Thursday _____

Friday _____

Saturday _____

Week In Review

What was your most joyful moment this week? What themes, new or already noted, did you find in your joy moments?

The subjects have a wonderful story to tell you. And if you follow the essence -- more joy and purpose will come to light. Keep exploring your joy and add discoveries to your joy library.

We don't need to improve ourselves, we just have to let go of what blocks our hearts.

- JACK KORNFIELD

{ finds joy in Buddhism }

Was any of your joy this week the product of working through fear and lessening your resistance towards a goal?

Recall scenarios where working through fear to reach a goal resulted in tremendous joy. With this awareness, in fearful moments you will find courage to move forward.

What were your achievements this week? Did you gain any new insights?

Note your most successful accomplishments, quality time with loved ones, and enlightening moments. Flip back periodically to honor your attentiveness to your priorities and review what you have learned.

Did you face challenges this week? Do you see different possibilities? How will you adjust moving forward?

Learning happens when you reflect and make adjustments to your course. Your growth is the product of working through struggles and finding a heart-centered solution. Joy resides here, too!

What kindness did you extend? How did you feel during and afterward?

Noting the kindness you extend during the week helps you to honor your light and love yourself more.

Use this space to begin planning for more joy in your life.

Dedicating time for joy makes your days brighter and more meaningful.

People

Places

Things

Experiences

Joy Date Ideas

Month No. 11 *Your Intentions*

YOUR KEYWORD

Along with your keyword, draw on the inner strength of curiosity, hope, and self-compassion as you approach your intentions.

Track the energy that you put towards your aspirations, and observe what is gained. Remember that being intentional about how you spend your time will help you achieve your goals. Where your attention goes, your energy flows.

No. 01
DESIRED GOAL:

ALCHEMY:

1	2	3	4	5	6	7
8	9	10	11	12	13	14
15	16	17	18	19	20	21
22	23	24	25	26	27	28
29	30	31				

No. 02
DESIRED GOAL:

ALCHEMY:

1	2	3	4	5	6	7
8	9	10	11	12	13	14
15	16	17	18	19	20	21
22	23	24	25	26	27	28
29	30	31				

No. 03
DESIRED GOAL:

ALCHEMY:

1	2	3	4	5	6	7
8	9	10	11	12	13	14
15	16	17	18	19	20	21
22	23	24	25	26	27	28
29	30	31				

No. 04
DESIRED GOAL:

ALCHEMY:

1	2	3	4	5	6	7
8	9	10	11	12	13	14
15	16	17	18	19	20	21
22	23	24	25	26	27	28
29	30	31				

Month In Review

Reflect on your time spent working towards your intentions.

Did you spend time as planned on your goals? Have you released what you needed to, and started to refine your focus? Record below a yes, partial, or no.

GOAL/ALCHEMY No. 01

GOAL/ALCHEMY No. 02

GOAL/ALCHEMY No. 03

GOAL/ALCHEMY No. 04

The key is not to prioritize your schedule but to schedule your priorities.
- STEVEN COVEY
{ found joy in principle centered living }

The yesses: Congratulations! Write about your successes.

How do you feel? What does this accomplishment offer you? If you no longer need to track this goal, consider introducing a new intention from your Month No. 1 exercise.

The partials: Is there anything new that you could implement that would help you achieve your goals?

Do you need to be more intentional in setting aside time for your desires? Do you need to break the goal down into smaller steps? Be kind to yourself as you process.

The Nos: What do you think prevented you? (Be as specific and honest as possible.)

Were there influences outside of your control? Were you resistant/how? Do you want to focus on this goal next month, or start a new one? All responses provide opportunities for growth.

Head to next month's intentions journal page (p.280) and write the goals and alchemy you will focus on for the next 30 days.

Month No. 11 *Your Free Space*

Create space for your dreams to materialize. As you journey, journal here about feelings, ideas, and next steps.

"I" Statements

Write positive and empowering messages.

Love

Eternity

Water Rest Area

Picnic Rest Area

Vista Rest Area

Month No. 12

Reflecting Upon Yourself

Know thyself.

- SOCRATES

{ found joy in philosophy }

You have turned the page towards your final destination! Take a few deep breaths to feel centered and present before you begin exploring the terrain of the closing chapter's summit. This month you will collect the final supportive essentials and decide about your future.

Imagine you are back on the light-filled path walking towards mile-marker No. 12 alongside the River of Authenticity. You notice this part of the woods is particularly tranquil and full of warmth. There is a quiet stillness in the air and more greenery than in any other part of the journey.

You spot lantern No. 12 just ahead, adjacent to a pond, and on a path that leads towards a sheltered oasis. There is a small fence crossing the path at this access in the trail juncture and a "no trespassing" sign. You are sure this route is indeed your path, and perhaps that sign is for everyone else. You step over the fence and continue forward onto a very narrow single-track trail. You look up and notice the tree branches creating a magical umbrella of shade. At this moment, the flowers that have been blooming alongside you on the path fill in ahead of you.

It feels as if you are entering a home. You take off your shoes to walk barefoot for the final few yards. Looking down to walk beside the flowers, you become more aware of the sensations beneath your feet. You notice that there are parts of the ground in this cove that feel very soft and parts that feel more worn. You experience a heightened sense of familiarity, a feeling that you have been here before.

As you enter the beautiful oasis that seems to be created just for you, among other luxuries, you see an elegant canopy bed with flowing white fabric panels. You set your travel bag down and rest your head on the bed's heart-shaped pillows delicately embroidered with your name. You close your eyes and drift off to sleep. In your dreams, you see a series of moments and significant people that made you who you are today. Once you wake up, you reflect on your dream. These noteworthy flashes were so telling that you don't want to forget them. You pull out your golden feather pen and write about each image. What do you write about?

You stand up slowly, ready to explore more; you notice a person that looks just like you, on a tree swing adorned with flowers, swaying back and forth in front of you. You are captivated by your mirror image. The person does not seem to notice you, but you are taking in everything about them. Again, you don't want to forget this extraordinary moment, so you pull out your golden feather pen and describe all that you are sensing about this person that looks just like you. What do you write?

Afterward, you set down your journal, and consider the rarity of this experience. First, in being fully present within such a radiantly love-filled setting tailored uniquely to you. Then, you contemplate how the forest showed you both the inside of you, through your dreams, and the outside of you, through your mirror image. You recall reading that life's journey is a continuously unwinding and evolving spiral, not a line. Your circular path weaves closer in towards your heart on each revolution. Over time your inner vibrations match your outer vibrations. You compare the inner and outer reflections of yourself, realizing what you can do to feel whole. You are now living a life of integrity, undivided, fully confident in your loving presence, and knowing who you are.

This month you will connect to your heart energy center, Anahata, to feel whole. The fourth chakra includes the "I" statements, "I love" and "I forgive."

I experienced being saturated in the expansive green heart chakra color while receiving a Healing Touch treatment outdoors in the countryside near Philadelphia. A fellow student was practicing what is known as the Spiral Meditation Technique, a sequence of hand movements created to open, connect, balance, and expand your energy system with a concentration on the heart. This experience helped me see our world is more than it appears.

F or the twelfth and final month of the journey, I encourage you to reflect on your journey both as a whole and as a part of the past twelve months. When writing about the entirety of you, consider the key moments and people in your life. How do you feel about them? What have you learned from them? What do you confidently know about yourself? Also, reflect on what you sensed from your heart about you on the swing. How are your inner and outer vibrations the same and different?

When writing about the past twelve months, reflect on what joy has revealed. How has joy expanded in your life? How have your intentions manifested, and how are they continuing to be realized? Reflect on what tools you gained, new practices you created, what you shed, and finally, your sense of purpose and state of wholeness.

While reflecting on any painful moments, look for the good that has occurred, and bless and release the hurtful parts. Set the intention to let go of the things that keep you confined and allow yourself to be who you are. From your reflection, point yourself in the direction of your desires. Look forward, and release doubts, self-criticism, and limitations. Discover and love your true self. Be available for your dreams and be you. Your purpose is to be love and flourish - in your beautiful uniqueness.

The desire to know your own soul will end all other desires.

- RUMI

{ found joy in the mystical }

WHAT YOU CAN GAIN FROM REFLECTION

Reflection can help you gain clarity, peace, and gratitude. Moreover, reflection can help you find more confidence and direction. For me, and perhaps for you too, reflection feels like a retrieval. The process helps you put the pieces of your life together. During reflection if you find yourself rehashing an undesirable repetitive life theme, consider practicing radical acceptance. Jon Kabat-Zinn famously penned, "Wherever You Go, There You Are." Or, as poet and novelist Rainer M. Rilke wrote, "Everyone, in the last analysis, experiences only one conflict in life which only disguises itself differently all the time." That essence is part of the thread of your life and can be lovingly regarded as the core issue you are working on in this lifetime. It is part of you, part of your alchemy, and part of your purpose. Refuge can be found from honoring your whole truth.

THE STEADFAST MESSAGE: LISTEN TO YOUR HEART, FOLLOW YOUR JOY, AND WITH CLEAR INTENTIONS EXPRESS YOUR TRUE SELF

There are two basic motivating forces: fear and love. When we are afraid, we pull back from life. When we are in love, we open to all that life has to offer with passion, excitement, and acceptance. We need to learn to love ourselves first, in all our glory and our imperfections. If we cannot love ourselves, we cannot fully open to our ability to love others or our potential to create. Evolution and all hopes for a better world rest in the fearlessness and open-hearted vision of people who embrace life.

- JOHN LENNON

{ found joy in peace }

The most important part of any story, and journey, could be how it ends. On a final note, you are loved and cherished. You matter. You count. You are seen and appreciated for who you are. You are here as you for a reason. Life supports you. And, you are directing all the moments of your story, through your choices. In this journey, you can either abandon your heart, or you can choose to stay in the vortex of its warm, wise, and majestic space. Do aspire to keep your heart open and choose love. *Trust in your innate goodness, your heart, and every part of your whole path.* When you choose from the love in your heart you are able to experience all of the freedom, connection, and expansion that comes along with being in the present moment. The magic that you find within the elevated present moment is part of you, just as you are a part of it. That magic is the joy connecting us all.

Your Personal 5-Star Review

⭐ ⭐ ⭐ ⭐ ⭐

Reflect upon the 10 best moments of your journey. Celebrate when you had the courage to follow your heart and your intuition, and you felt the elevating magic of joy.

1.

2.

3.

4.

5.

6.

7.

8.

9.

10.

You are a brilliant being. Spread your wings wide and light up your path. Your power is within you.

Week No. 49 *Your Joy*

Cultivate joy! | Schedule something on your bucket list!

Record moments of joy each day

What was your joy? Who/What gave rise to the joy? What did it feel, look, taste, smell, or sound like?

The process of reflective writing supports awareness. Awareness of what brings you joy serves as a heart-centered, resourceful compass, and unfolds more joy. The key to the journey is recognizing, understanding, and following -- your personal joy.

Joy Date · Write about your joy date - what you explored and how you felt.

_____

Sunday _____

_____

Monday _____

_____

Tuesday _____

_____

Wednesday _____

_____

Thursday _____

_____

Friday _____

_____

Saturday _____

_____

Week In Review

What was your most joyful moment this week? What themes, new or already noted, did you find in your joy moments?

The subjects have a wonderful story to tell you. And if you follow the essence -- more joy and purpose will come to light. Keep exploring your joy and add discoveries to your joy library.

Was any of your joy this week the product of working through fear and lessening your resistance towards a goal?

Recall scenarios where working through fear to reach a goal resulted in tremendous joy. With this awareness, in fearful moments you will find courage to move forward.

What were your achievements this week? Did you gain any new insights?

Note your most successful accomplishments, quality time with loved ones, and enlightening moments. Flip back periodically to honor your attentiveness to your priorities and review what you have learned.

Did you face challenges this week? Do you see different possibilities? How will you adjust moving forward?

Learning happens when you reflect and make adjustments to your course. Your growth is the product of working through struggles and finding a heart-centered solution. Joy resides here, too!

What kindness did you extend? How did you feel during and afterward?

Noting the kindness you extend during the week helps you to honor your light and love yourself more.

Use this space to begin planning for more joy in your life.

Dedicating time for joy makes your days brighter and more meaningful.

People

Places

Things

Experiences

Joy Date Ideas

Week No. 50 *Your Joy*

Cultivate joy!

Thank someone for making a positive difference in your day!

Record moments of joy each day

What was your joy? Who/What gave rise to the joy? What did it feel, look, taste, smell, or sound like?

The process of reflective writing supports awareness. Awareness of what brings you joy serves as a heart-centered, resourceful compass, and unfolds more joy. The key to the journey is recognizing, understanding, and following -- your personal joy.

Joy Date · Write about your joy date - what you explored and how you felt.

Sunday _____

Monday _____

Tuesday _____

Wednesday _____

Thursday _____

Friday _____

Saturday _____

Week In Review

What was your most joyful moment this week? What themes, new or already noted, did you find in your joy moments?

The subjects have a wonderful story to tell you. And if you follow the essence -- more joy and purpose will come to light. Keep exploring your joy and add discoveries to your joy library.

Was any of your joy this week the product of working through fear and lessening your resistance towards a goal?

Recall scenarios where working through fear to reach a goal resulted in tremendous joy. With this awareness, in fearful moments you will find courage to move forward.

What were your achievements this week? Did you gain any new insights?

Note your most successful accomplishments, quality time with loved ones, and enlightening moments. Flip back periodically to honor your attentiveness to your priorities and review what you have learned.

Did you face challenges this week? Do you see different possibilities? How will you adjust moving forward?

Learning happens when you reflect and make adjustments to your course. Your growth is the product of working through struggles and finding a heart-centered solution. Joy resides here, too!

What kindness did you extend? How did you feel during and afterward?

Noting the kindness you extend during the week helps you to honor your light and love yourself more.

Use this space to begin planning for more joy in your life.

Dedicating time for joy makes your days brighter and more meaningful.

People

Places

Things

Experiences

Joy Date Ideas

Week No. 51 — Your Joy

Cultivate joy! | When you hear your discouraging voice remember to leave yourself alone!

Record moments of joy each day | What was your joy? Who/What gave rise to the joy? What did it feel, look, taste, smell, or sound like?

The process of reflective writing supports awareness. Awareness of what brings you joy serves as a heart-centered, resourceful compass, and unfolds more joy. The key to the journey is recognizing, understanding, and following -- your personal joy.

Joy Date · Write about your joy date - what you explored and how you felt.

Sunday _____

Monday _____

Tuesday _____

Wednesday _____

Thursday _____

Friday _____

Saturday _____

Week In Review

What was your most joyful moment this week? What themes, new or already noted, did you find in your joy moments?

The subjects have a wonderful story to tell you. And if you follow the essence -- more joy and purpose will come to light. Keep exploring your joy and add discoveries to your joy library.

Joy is prayer. Joy is strength. Joy is love. Joy is a net of love by which you can catch souls.

- MOTHER TERESA

{ found joy in service }

Was any of your joy this week the product of working through fear and lessening your resistance towards a goal?

Recall scenarios where working through fear to reach a goal resulted in tremendous joy. With this awareness, in fearful moments you will find courage to move forward.

What were your achievements this week? Did you gain any new insights?

Note your most successful accomplishments, quality time with loved ones, and enlightening moments. Flip back periodically to honor your attentiveness to your priorities and review what you have learned.

Did you face challenges this week? Do you see different possibilities? How will you adjust moving forward?

Learning happens when you reflect and make adjustments to your course. Your growth is the product of working through struggles and finding a heart-centered solution. Joy resides here, too!

What kindness did you extend? How did you feel during and afterward?

Noting the kindness you extend during the week helps you to honor your light and love yourself more.

Use this space to begin planning for more joy in your life.

Dedicating time for joy makes your days brighter and more meaningful.

People

Places

Things

Experiences

Joy Date Ideas

Week No. 52 *Your Joy*

Cultivate joy! | Share what you have discovered that has changed your life!

Record moments of joy each day | What was your joy? Who/What gave rise to the joy? What did it feel, look, taste, smell, or sound like?

The process of reflective writing supports awareness. Awareness of what brings you joy serves as a heart-centered, resourceful compass, and unfolds more joy. The key to the journey is recognizing, understanding, and following -- your personal joy.

Joy Date · Write about your joy date - what you explored and how you felt.

_____

Sunday _____

Monday _____

Tuesday _____

Wednesday _____

Thursday _____

Friday _____

Saturday _____

Week In Review

What was your most joyful moment this week? What themes, new or already noted, did you find in your joy moments?

The subjects have a wonderful story to tell you. And if you follow the essence -- more joy and purpose will come to light. Keep exploring your joy and add discoveries to your joy library.

Was any of your joy this week the product of working through fear and lessening your resistance towards a goal?

Recall scenarios where working through fear to reach a goal resulted in tremendous joy. With this awareness, in fearful moments you will find courage to move forward.

What were your achievements this week? Did you gain any new insights?

Note your most successful accomplishments, quality time with loved ones, and enlightening moments. Flip back periodically to honor your attentiveness to your priorities and review what you have learned.

Did you face challenges this week? Do you see different possibilities? How will you adjust moving forward?

Learning happens when you reflect and make adjustments to your course. Your growth is the product of working through struggles and finding a heart-centered solution. Joy resides here, too!

What kindness did you extend? How did you feel during and afterward?

Noting the kindness you extend during the week helps you to honor your light and love yourself more.

Use this space to begin planning for more joy in your life.

Dedicating time for joy makes your days brighter and more meaningful.

People

Places

Things

Experiences

Joy Date Ideas

Your Intentions

YOUR KEYWORD

Along with your keyword, draw on the inner strength of curiosity, hope, and self-compassion as you approach your intentions.

Track the energy that you put towards your aspirations, and observe what is gained. Remember that being intentional about how you spend your time will help you achieve your goals. Where your attention goes, your energy flows.

No. 01

DESIRED GOAL:

ALCHEMY:

1	2	3	4	5	6	7
8	9	10	11	12	13	14
15	16	17	18	19	20	21
22	23	24	25	26	27	28
29	30	31				

No. 02

DESIRED GOAL:

ALCHEMY:

1	2	3	4	5	6	7
8	9	10	11	12	13	14
15	16	17	18	19	20	21
22	23	24	25	26	27	28
29	30	31				

No. 03

DESIRED GOAL:

ALCHEMY:

1	2	3	4	5	6	7
8	9	10	11	12	13	14
15	16	17	18	19	20	21
22	23	24	25	26	27	28
29	30	31				

No. 04

DESIRED GOAL:

ALCHEMY:

1	2	3	4	5	6	7
8	9	10	11	12	13	14
15	16	17	18	19	20	21
22	23	24	25	26	27	28
29	30	31				

Month In Review

The power of intention
is the power to manifest, to
create, to live a life of unlimited
abundance, and to attract into
your life the right people at
the right moments.

- WAYNE DYER
{ found joy in
self-empowerment }

Reflect on your time spent working towards your intentions.

Did you spend time as planned on your goals? Have you released what you needed to, and started to refine your focus? Record below a yes, partial, or no.

GOAL/ALCHEMY No. 01

GOAL/ALCHEMY No. 02

GOAL/ALCHEMY No. 03

GOAL/ALCHEMY No. 04

The yesses: Congratulations! Write about your successes.

How do you feel? What does this accomplishment offer you? If you no longer need to track this goal, consider introducing a new intention from your Month No. 1 exercise.

The partials: Is there anything new that you could implement that would help you achieve your goals?

Do you need to be more intentional in setting aside time for your desires? Do you need to break the goal down into smaller steps? Be kind to yourself as you process.

The Nos: What do you think prevented you? (Be as specific and honest as possible.)

Were there influences outside of your control? Were you resistant/how? Do you want to focus on this goal next month, or start a new one? All responses provide opportunities for growth.

Month No. 12 *Your Free Space*

Create space for your dreams to materialize. As you journey, journal here about feelings, ideas, and next steps.

"I" Statements

Write positive and empowering messages.

You are...

adaptable, appreciative, aware, balanced, caring, communicative, connected, courageous, creative, curious, dedicated, disciplined, effective, empathetic, fervent, focused, forgiving, full of laughter, generous, grateful, harmonious, heart-centered, honest, hopeful, innovative, inspiring, intuitive, loving, passionate, patient, perseverant, positive, present, respectful, responsible, strong, smart, strategic, supportive, thoughtful, trustworthy, unique, understanding, wise, and true to yourself.

what is your
JOY?

Reference Guide *Your Joy Library*

As you journey and learn more about your joy, index what you discover creates the experience in your life. You will have a large collection of ideas to draw from when you need to lift your spirit.

People:

Places:

Things:

Experiences:

Epilogue

The privilege of a lifetime is to become who you truly are.

- C. G. JUNG

{ found joy in psychology }

In the Spring of 2016, in the depths of my unease, I attended a Healing Touch Level 3 training class in my beautiful college hometown of Boulder, Colorado. While receiving an energy treatment from a fellow student, I saw myself peacefully floating in the current of a river; a pen was placed into my hand, indicating that I was to write. The fruition of *Flourish* marks the manifestation of that vision.

I wrote the first drafts of this book in the Spring and Summer of 2020. While writing, the river of my life felt choppy. I was uneasy because of what was happening in parts of my personal life and empathic to what was transpiring in the world as a whole. Writing openly was also touching upon sensitivities and pain. My writing forced me to do some unexpected processing, merge with my pain, and practice radical acceptance. I proceeded with the project because these are the tools that keep me afloat in any currents. Sharing my story and healing path felt like something I was meant to do, as if it was part of my purpose. I am so pleased that I pushed through my discomfort because as the book developed, I developed. I witnessed a significant inner transformation in self-awareness, gained trust in my life, and felt newfound gratitude for being alive. I accepted all the parts of my dream and myself, and in a miraculously enlightening way, I found my truth.

As for my intentions shared in Month No.1, and the opportunities shared in Month No. 3, it was at the start of the second round of drafting the book that I started sitting in meditation for 15 minutes most days. I heard/saw each opening chapter's guided meditation. I gained clarity. That inner vision influenced my sense of heartfelt confidence too. I believe adding meditations and their illustrations strengthened the book. As I continued to meditate and write, I found more clarity and confidence. New ideas, words, and references appeared within me that I am certain were guided by God/the Universe. Creating this book allowed me to thread fragmented parts of my life together, make sense of my experiences, and see more of my full potential. In addition to getting comfortable meditating daily for an extended period of time, I had to work through my fears about time while creating for many x many x many ^ countless hours (math equation joke). That feeling has subsided. I reduced the weight of my self-doubt about my abilities to write a personal growth book from a 9 to a 0 and the weight of feeling I don't have enough time to succeed with my aspirations from 7 to 0. I have grown in clarity, heartfelt confidence, and faith.

The journey we traveled together is a beacon of joy for me. I hope that my love transfers just like light and that you feel closer to your truth, more joyful, and more alive. I hope that you are more forgiving, more resilient, and experiencing more beauty in your life. I hope that you are more intentional, realizing your dreams, and the remainder of your desires are on their way to you. I hope that you feel more love inside yourself, feel true to yourself, and that you are embracing your wholeness.

It is fulfilling and meaningful to hear from people who have benefited from my work, and our work together. I encourage you to share how the journey positively influenced your path. I also invite you to take another adventure for the next 365 days and continue to flourish with another guidebook in your hands. You will find more truth and joy, remain focused on what is truly important to you, and see aspects of your life from a new perspective. Cultivate and chronicle another year of your beautiful life. Just begin again, and continue to move forward towards the richness of your full potential.

Namaste

I honor the place in you in which the entire universe dwells.
I honor the place in you which is of love, of truth,
of light, and of peace.
When you are in that place in you,
and I am in that place in me, we are one.

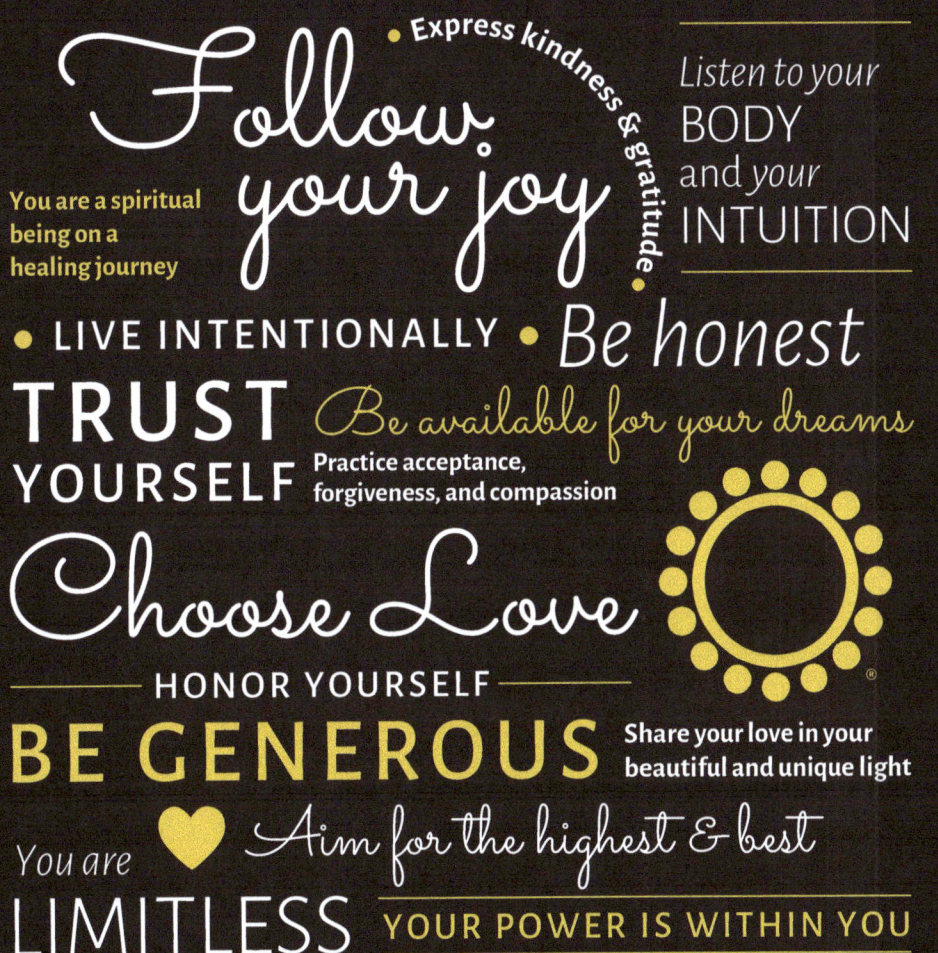

Express kindness & gratitude.

Follow your joy

You are a spiritual being on a healing journey

Listen to your BODY and *your* INTUITION

LIVE INTENTIONALLY • Be honest

TRUST YOURSELF

Be available for your dreams

Practice acceptance, forgiveness, and compassion

Choose Love

HONOR YOURSELF

BE GENEROUS

Share your love in your beautiful and unique light

You are LIMITLESS

Aim for the highest & best

YOUR POWER IS WITHIN YOU

Closing Gratitude

Eventually you will come to understand that
love heals everything, and love is all there is.

- GARY ZUKAV

{ finds joy in transformation }

I have much gratitude to express.

Thank you to my friends Jana Bricker and Thomas Skelter for introducing me to Michelle Fiordaliso. Michelle, thank you for coaching me in your unique way, recommending the *Life-Changing Magic of Tidying Up* and *The Artist's Way*, and urging me to return to the place where I veered from my center.

Thank you to Marie Kondo and Julia Cameron. Your work has shaped my life and this book. Thank you to Mark Nepo. You help me better comprehend the river running through my life.

Thank you to the Healing Touch Program, and the founder Janet Mentgen, for your structured and lengthy education on the skills of energy healing. I am confident in energy work because of the depth of knowledge the program offers. The mutual intention statement for healing has positively influenced my life and work in a way I never imagined possible.

Thank you to my Healing Touch mentor, Heather Lenox. You go the extra mile to support your mentees and, for that, I am grateful. And thank you to Diana Czekaiski, my Reiki teacher. I appreciate the light atmosphere you create in your close knit classes. Incorporating the energy of Reiki noticeably strengthens healing work.

Thank you, Bernie Bugg, for your inspiring words in the woods. You influenced the beautiful trail within. I hope you know that wherever you are now, on the other side of the veil.

Thank you, Rosie Accola, for your editing expertise. Your writing support refined my thoughts and words in a way I could not do alone. I am truly grateful for your guidance as we circled this book and my life by extension.

Thank you, Jamie Andrzejewski, owner of Nourish Natural Products, Flourish Integral Health's essential oil blend production partner. Thank you for your smart contributions to the Raising Your Vibration chapter, your encouragement, and your essential oil expertise.

Thank you, Jenn Kippert, for your talented graphic artistry. I appreciate your inventiveness and patience as we worked together to design this book to look and feel just as I wanted it to be. The final compilation is joy.

Thank you, Libby Ozog, for your illustrations. Your pen and ink drawings brought the book to life in a way that I could not have fully anticipated. You did a brilliant job at taking my images and rough sketches and creating beautiful artwork.

Thank you to the suppliers of Flourish Integral Health. Your high-quality materials make the products sparkle.

Thank you to my customers and clients. I am grateful for you.

Thank you to my dear friends for your supportive presence, encouragement, and laughter. I am blessed by you and the joy you bring to my life. I hope you all see the love you reflect to me in *Flourish*. A special thank you to early readers, and listeners, you helped form the book and aid my healing process.

Thank you, Janet Greif, for your life-line counsel, strong belief in me, and constant encouragement to walk a path to my true self. You are a guiding light.

To my parents, Peter and Joan, thank you for your life-long caring support, strength, and wisdom. Your love is steadfast.

To my kids, Brandon and Pierson, I love you so much. You give my life purpose. You are both amazingly independent thinkers, and excellent at expressing your true selves.

To God/the Universe, thank you for working through me.

And to myself, the one who is always searching, dreaming, and reaching, I wrote this for you too, so that you will forever have a clear and flourishing path in your beautiful life.

Notes

The How and Why of Flourish

1. Whyte, David (2009) *The Three Marriages: Reimagining Work, Self and Relationships*, Riverhead Hardcover.

2. Tayor, Steve (2021) *Extraordinary Awakenings: When Trauma Leads to Transformation*, New World Library, pp. 179.

3. Egnew, Danielle (2014) *Daily Spiritual Insight: 365 Lessons for Lifetime Growth*, Create Space/Call to Light Press, Day 116.

4. Paul, Nina L., PhD (2006) *Reiki for Dummies*, Wiley Publishing, Inc., pp. 114.

The How and Why of Joy

5. content.time.com/time/magazine/article/0,9171,1015863-3,00.html

The How and Why of Intention

6. Rubin, Gretchen (2015) *The Happiness Project: Or Why I Spent a Year Trying to Sing in the Morning, Clean My Closets, Fight Right, Read Aristotle, and Generally Have More Fun*, Harper Paperback.

Visioning Your Aim

7. Cameron, Julia (1992) *The Artist's Way: A Spiritual Path to Higher Creativity*, Tarcher/Putnam, pp. 92.

8. Nepo, Mark (2012) *Seven Thousand Ways to Listen: Staying Close to What is Sacred*, Atria, An Imprint of Simon & Schuster, pp. 103.

Water Rest Stop

9. https://www.webmd.com/diet/features/6-reasons-to-drink-water#

10. Williams, Anthony (2016) *Life-Changing Foods: Save Yourself and the Ones you Love with the Hidden Healing Powers of Fruits & Vegetables*, Hay House, Inc., pp. 94, 142.

11. Emoto, Masaru (2005) *The Hidden Messages in Water*: Atria Books.

12. Taggert, Lynne (2017) *The Power of Eight: Harnessing the Miraculous Energy of a Small Group to Heal Others, Your Life, and the World*, Atria, An Imprint of Simon & Schuster, pp. 45-46.

Caring For Yourself

13. https://locallove.ca/issues/the-revolutionary-origins-of-self-care/#.X2K_ly2ZOZI

Manifesting a Whole Perspective

14. https://blog.yogamatters.com/the-meaning-behind-108/

15. Askinose,v Heather and Jandro, Timmi (2017) *Crystal Muse: Everyday Rituals to Tune into the Real You*, Hay House, Inc., pp. 89, 125.

16. Iyengar, B.K.S (1976) *Light On Yoga: The Bible of Modern Yoga*, Schocken Books, pp. 441.

Your Midway Celebration

17. Oprah.com, September 2012 issue

18. Mable Hoffman (1980) *Appetizers*, H.P. Books, pp. 119.

Journaling to Connect

19. Adams, Kathleen (1990) *Journal to the Self: Twenty-Two Paths to Personal Growth*, Grand Central Publishing, pp.37.

Communing with an Altar

20. https://en.m.wikipedia.org/wiki/Pedulum

Feeling Safe and Grounded

21. https://www.healthline.com/health/grounding

22. https://www.greggbraden.com/meditation-inner-peace-and-calm/

Additional Resources

In addition to the resources referenced within *Flourish*, here is a list of reading that I have found enlightening on my journey. Please visit my website for other *Soulful Reads* book recommendations.

Understanding Aromatherapy

Dr. Johnson, Scott A. (2015) *Evidence-Based Essential Oil Therapy: The Ultimate Guide to Therapeutic and Clinical Application of Essentials Oils*, Scott A. Johnson Professional Writing Services, LLC.

Life Science (2019) *Essential Oils Desk Reference Eighth Edition*, Life Science Publishing.

Understanding the Art of Expression

Nepo, Mark (2019) *Drinking From the River of Light: The Life of Expression*, Sounds True.

Understanding Dreams

Cooper, D. Jason (1996) *The Power of Dreaming: Messages from Your Inner Self*, Llewellyn Publications.

Understanding Healing Work

Brennan, Barbara (1988) *Hands of Light: A Guide to Healing Through the Human Energy Field*, Bantam Books.

Dr. Chopra, Deepak (2015) *Quantum Healing: Exploring the Frontiers of Mind/Body Medicine*, Bantam Books.

Taylor, Madisyn (2018) *Unmedicated: The Four Pillars of Natural Wellness*, Atria Books, An Imprint of Simon & Schuster, Inc.

Understanding Intuition

Chestney, Kim (2020) *Radical Intuition: A Revolutionary Guide to Using Your Inner Power*, New World Library.

Understanding the Journey

Coelho, Paulo (2014) *The Alchemist: A Fable About Following Your Dream*, Harper One.

Medcalf, Joshua (2015) *Chop Wood Carry Water: How to Fall in Love with the Process of Becoming Great*, Create Space Independent Publishing Platform.

Ruiz, Don Miguel (1997) *The Four Agreements: A Practical Guide to Personal Freedom*, Amber-Allen Publishing.

Understanding Joy

Lama, Dalai, Tutu, Desmond, Abrams, Douglas (2016) *The Book of Joy: Lasting Happiness in a Changing World*, Avery, An Imprint of Penguin Random House, LLC.

Understanding Pause

Raheem, Octavia F. (2022) *Pause, Rest, Be: Stillness Practices for Courage in Times of Change*, Shambhala.

Understanding Presence

Tolle, Eckhart (2001) *The Power of Now: A Guide to Spiritual Enlightenment*, New World Library.

Understanding Unhealthy Relationships

Carnes, Patrick (2019) *The Betrayal Bond: Breaking Free of Exploitive Relationships*, Health Communications, Inc.

Evans, Patrica (2010) *The Verbally Abusive Relationship: How to Stop Being Abused and How to Stop Abusing*, Adams Media.

Understanding Yourself

Myss, Caroline (2013) *Archetypes: Who are you?*, Hay House, LLC.

Kiersey, David, Bates, Marilyn (1984) *Please Understand Me: Character & Temperament Types*, Gnosology Books Ltd.

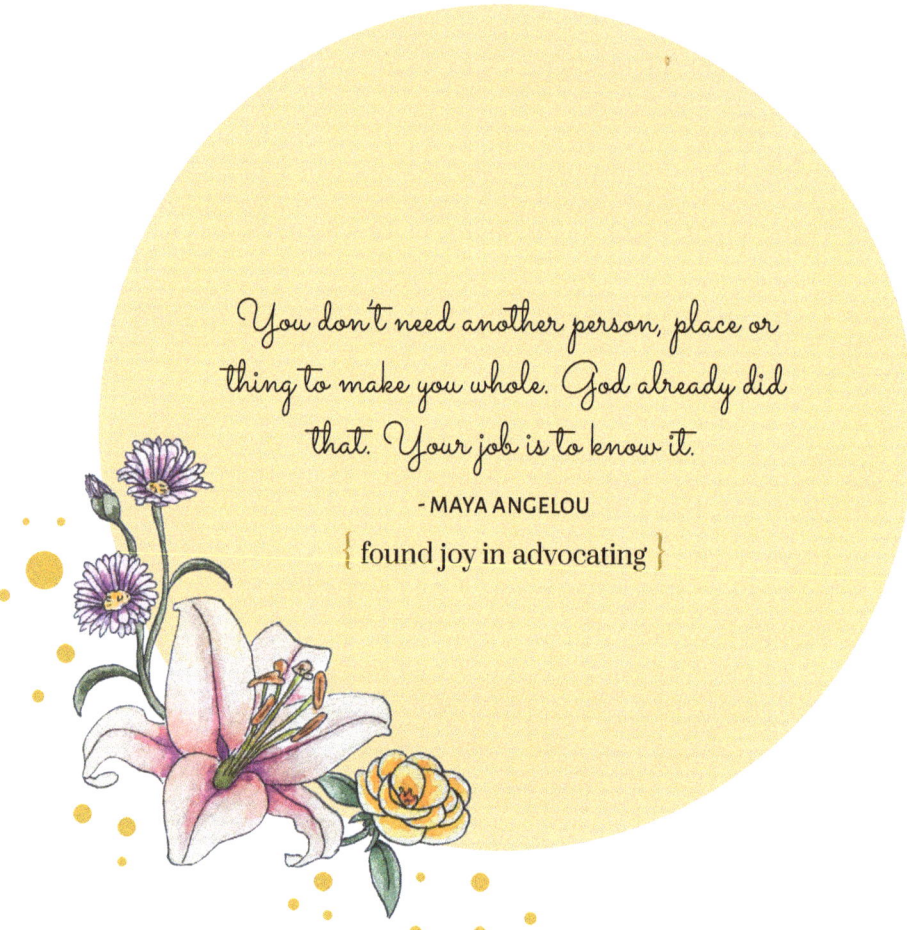

You don't need another person, place or thing to make you whole. God already did that. Your job is to know it.

- MAYA ANGELOU

{ found joy in advocating }

About the Author

Allison McCabe Bruce is an intuitive Energy Medicine practitioner, intentional healing jewelry artist, conscious product designer, and writer. As founder of Flourish Integral Health, Allison offers healing products and services to help you flourish on your personal growth journey to whole health. She is also a columnist for *Energy Magazine*, author of Soulful Reads.

She learned the value of strategy and structure for meaningful change in her construction management career. In a leadership role for Fortune 500 companies, she directed diverse teams accountable for development, design, and implementation of corporate real estate solutions across the United States and Canada.

A time of despair followed by the pursuit of joy, led Allison to develop her creative abilities and redirect her career focus to the healing arts. She is an entrepreneur at heart. Her first company was a line of children's clothing with a celebrity sighting on *The Oprah Winfrey Show*.

Allison is a Healing Touch Certified Practitioner, Reiki Master Practitioner, devoted yogi with a teaching certification in Hatha yoga, and holds a BS in Architectural Engineering with an emphasis in Construction Management from the University of Colorado, Boulder.

She resides in suburban Chicago, Illinois. She is mom to Brandon and Pierson.

Find her at www.flourishintegralhealth.com and on Instagram @flourishintegralhealth.